# THE FLIGHT HOME

NINE JOURNEYS - NINE LESSONS

# VERONICA LLORCA–SMITH

The Flight Home

By Veronica Llorca-Smith

ISBN-13: 978-988-8843-42-8

© 2023 Veronica Llorca-Smith

Cover photo by George Papadopoulos

BIOGRAPHY & AUTOBIOGRAPHY

EB206

All rights reserved. No part of this book may be reproduced in material form, by any means, whether graphic, electronic, mechanical or other, including photocopying or information storage, in whole or in part. May not be used to prepare other publications without written permission from the publisher except in the case of brief quotations embodied in critical articles or reviews. For information contact info@earnshawbooks.com

Published in Hong Kong by Earnshaw Books Ltd.

## Dedication

In the memory of my late dad, who taught me that the currency of life is time.
Inspired by my mom, who taught me that anything is possible, and by my sister Vicky's contagious laugh.
Dedicated to the love of my life Dave, and to Alba and Maia, the precious gifts of motherhood.

# CHAPTER ONE
## *Locked Abroad – Flexibility*

It was almost midnight on August 15th, 2021. The Cathay Pacific flight attendant had just announced that boarding was about to begin, and I had five minutes to organize our hand-carry bags and jump into the queue with Alba and Maia. Smiling at my phone, I sent a message to Dave from my iPhone, 'About to board. See you in 3 weeks. Love you. Your girls.'

I stretched my arms sideways and checked on the girls. They were both asleep on the dark blue chairs, awkwardly leaning their little heads against their shoulders. I shook them gently to wake them and whispered, 'Alba, Maia, we are going to Spain. The plane is leaving. Who wants to see Grandma and all the family?'

They barely moved. I adjusted my light pink watch on my right wrist and started converting our trip into hours. Twelve hours from Hong Kong to Frankfurt, followed by a stopover, and five hours from Frankfurt to Tenerife. That was only the first part. I took a deep breath, thinking about the long trip ahead as a solo parent with my purple suitcase and my two grumpy little monkeys.

I hadn't seen my family in two years. Would Mom recognize the girls? Would I be able to keep the trip a surprise from my

# THE FLIGHT HOME

family back in the Canary Islands? I imagined my 82-year-old grandma's face when she saw her great-granddaughters walk through the door of her old house. I discreetly wiped a tear, knowing it was worth the effort.

A few minutes later, we were in the passengers queue waving goodbye to Hong Kong through the airport window. Alba and Maia were both dressed in identical pink hoodies. They were almost the same height and looked like twins. Holding hands, they repeated one after the other, 'Bye, bye Hong Kong, bye, bye Daddy, bye, bye Django, night, night moon, and airplanes.' We entered the 747 airplane, not knowing that this flight was about to change our lives.

As soon as we took off, I looked through the window as Hong Kong became smaller and smaller until it finally disappeared under the clouds. I closed my eyes and traveled back in time, going through the past 18 months. How could our lives have changed so much, so quickly?

In January 2020, not even two years earlier, we were on the Gold Coast in Australia, celebrating New Year with Dave's family, when news of a lethal virus from China started to make the headlines around the world. At first, the general public naively thought it was a China-only pandemic as we watched the images on TV in disbelief. The epicenter of the virus in Wuhan was in lockdown for weeks in a row, and thousands of patients were dying in overcrowded hospitals or locked up in their homes without any medical help. The streets looked deserted, and the government limited basic individual freedom of movement and enforced curfews. It looked very different from the hectic city I had visited years before for my work when I was living in China.

Soon we would learn that the virus didn't respect borders, spreading to other countries, leaving devastation and death behind. The pandemic hit Europe, and I often thought of my former colleagues in Italy, particularly Bergamo, when I watched the footage of people confined to their homes singing from their balconies. Many applauded public health workers on their way to work, while hundreds were dying daily in hospitals, some without any care, due to the lack of resources and ventilators.

Back home in Hong Kong, just like in all the other countries, the pandemic hit hard, and the government reacted quickly. In a matter of days, schools, public spaces, beaches, and clubs were shut down. Restaurants were allowed to operate until 6:00 p.m. with major restrictions and a limit of four guests per table, and the local authorities enforced the mask mandate for all individuals from the age of two. The measures lasted for months in a row, with little steps of progress quickly annulated by even stricter rules. Our little flat in the neighborhood of Kennedy Town became everything to us — a kindergarten with online classes, an office with back-to-back calls in the girls' bedroom, a play area, and everything else in between.

Alba and Maia didn't know any better and became used to grabbing their Hello Kitty masks before leaving the house, which was becoming less frequent. The parks and playgrounds were closed, and we walked doing loops around them, looking at the empty slides and swings, sealed with red and white tape. Alba often asked me, 'Mommy, when will the park open again? I want to go to the monkey bars.'

I dreaded that question. I always told her the truth, so, with a bitter smile, I replied, 'I don't know Alba, but I hope very soon.' Not happy with my answer, she asked me again and again until I distracted her with candy or a singing bird. That was the reality of growing up during the pandemic for a four-year-old. I had no idea when she would, without a mask on, be able to push her little sister on the swing again or ride a bike.

Life was becoming difficult for all of us. The restrictions were becoming unreasonable, and the police started to fine cyclists without masks and scold parents about their toddlers not wearing them properly. In April 2020, the government decided to lock the border by imposing an inhumane quarantine of 21 days in a hotel room for all inbound international travelers and returning residents. We were allowed to leave but wouldn't be able to return unless we wanted to endure weeks of isolation to manage the risk of testing positive and being sent to public facilities for further isolation. 'We will never do that to our daughters,' Dave protested, visibly angry, as we read the news in the newspaper. I nodded in frustration.

The months passed slowly, and the city became grey. Spring became summer, which turned into autumn, and soon one year had gone by without any change in the colors of our life. It was still grey. Expats started to flee the city, and Dave and I saw our friends depart one after the other. Some returned to their home countries, others moved to Singapore, and many decided to leave with a one-way ticket not knowing if they would ever come up. We said goodbye to our friends on the phone because group gatherings were not allowed, and the farewells never happened. Where was the Hong Kong I had fallen in love with when I moved to the vibrant city in 2007? Would it ever be the same again? Our favorite restaurants started to close without notice. First SOLAS, where Dave and I had had our first kiss, then Oola, where we had had our first date, and finally, the iconic Staunton's Bar on Elgin Street, where all expats used to hang out in the trendy neighborhood of Mid-Levels. There was little left of Asia's World City and every day a new piece was taken away.

In early 2021, the government started improvising quarantine facilities for those considered close contacts of positive cases, even if they had tested negative and showed no symptoms. The punishment was a strict three-week isolation in a remote location called Penny's Bay on Lantau Island. The area was occupied by dozens of shipping containers one next to the other in perfect symmetry. The units had been converted into dark and depressing individual cubicles with small toilets and a sealed window. The doors remained locked at all times except when the food was delivered. Ironically Penny's Bay was only a couple of kilometers from Disneyland, *The Happiest Place on Earth*. Whoever had planned all of this had a dark sense of humor. We hoped it was all exaggerations and rumours from the media, as it didn't seem sensible to lock people up, including children, for 21 days inside a container without fresh air or any type of ventilation. A few weeks later, our first friends were sent in.

'Check this out,' Dave said one morning, handing his phone to me. I brought the screen closer and saw a heat map of Hong Kong with many red dots across different parts of the city. I zoomed in, and the red dots were everywhere. I looked at him, puzzled, and he continued, 'they are now tracking down all the positive cases, and if a building has a confirmed case, it will be evacuated, and all residents will be sent to Penny's Bay for the 21-day sentence.'

'We should get out of here. It's getting scary,' I replied, looking at Alba and Maia, who were playing on the floor. Dave didn't say anything. We both knew leaving was not an option because we wouldn't be able to return, and our life was here, our flat, our jobs, our puppy Django. Hong Kong was home.

A week later, in April 2021, my best friend Ingrid sent me a message. We had planned to meet that day for lunch, and I thought she was texting to confirm the restaurant. Instead, the message said, 'I'm a close contact of someone who tested positive at my gym. I think they are going to send us all to Penny's Bay. Call you later. x.'

I felt the shivers in my body. I knew parents were separated

# THE FLIGHT HOME

from their babies if they tested positive, and I immediately imagined the worst. Ingrid had a two-year-old and was still breastfeeding baby Tommy. I kept my phone nearby that afternoon, checking the screen every few minutes, and suddenly the dreaded message popped up. 'They are coming in one hour to take us all. We are getting ready to go to Penny's Bay. This is shocking.'

I read the message again, staring at the screen in silence. My best friend was living a mother's worst nightmare. It could have been me. It could still be me at any time, any day. Her family was sent away with one suitcase each. Little Alex spent his third birthday locked up in the container, but no one told him it was his special day to avoid a toddler's meltdown. There was no birthday cake, no birthday wish. After three days in isolation, Ingrid tested positive and was sent to Queen Mary Hospital alone, leaving her partner and the boys behind. She called me crying, 'I won't be able to breastfeed Tommy. What happens if we all test positive? Who will look after him? The government will take him.'

I felt the panic in her shaky voice. I looked at Alba and Maia, who were playing with their Paw Patrol toys in their bedroom, and I improvised the best answer I could, 'That's not going to happen, but if you all test positive and he doesn't, I will join him in quarantine. He can't be alone, and I know you would do the same for us.'

Luckily for both of us, that never happened, but Tommy remained locked up without the warm cuddles from his mom for almost a month before they could finally be reunited. In the following weeks, other friends were sent to Penny's Bay, and we all had a suitcase ready at home with some basics like chargers, a comfortable pillow, toilet paper, and chocolate in case it was our turn.

## VERONICA LLORCA-SMITH

One Monday morning in August 2021, Dave was reading the South China Morning Post and excitedly announced that Hong Kong had reduced the quarantine upon arrival from 21 to 7 days. It was the best news we had received in 18 months and sounded like a fantastic opportunity to travel overseas. Being isolated for only a week ironically felt like freedom now.

Dave spontaneously added, 'You and the girls should go. Jump on a plane tomorrow; you should take advantage and spend a month with your family in Spain. Just go and do it before it changes again. You will regret it if you don't.'

My head was spinning. 'I don't know,' I replied, with a hesitant smile. 'I think I have developed the Stockholm syndrome after almost two years trapped here.' Traveling overseas by myself with the girls was not something I was considering, despite all the traveling I had previously done in my life. I felt comfortable in my small Hong Kong bubble, and the thought of going overseas frightened me. Anything could change anytime.

Using all sorts of arguments, Dave insisted until I gave in. The more I thought about seeing my family, having my girls play with their cousins in Spanish, and hug their great-grandma, the more I embraced the adventure. Even though my sixth sense warned me something was off, it was worth the risk, and three days later, on August 15th, 2021, I was packing my purple suitcase, ready to travel for the first time in almost two years.

The trip was long, and the jet lag was unbearable, especially as I had barely slept during the flight, but we had made it to Tenerife, where the skies were deep blue, and the sun was shining, just like it did 40 years earlier when the islands were my home. I was back to my roots. After the first night at the hotel, I woke up in the dark at 5:00 a.m. and grabbed my phone to check the Hong Kong news, which had become an obsession. I clicked on the South China Morning Post app, and my heart started to

## THE FLIGHT HOME

beat faster when I read that there was a new wave of infection cases and Hong Kong was toughening the measures. They were again imposing 21 days of mandatory quarantine upon arrival in Hong Kong with immediate effect. It was a shock. Had the news broken one day earlier, I would not have jumped on that plane. Dave and I had always agreed that a quarantine of 21 days was not an option for the girls. We worried about the psychological impact of prolonged isolation, the lack of social interaction, and the deprivation of sunlight and fresh air on children. Thinking of Ingrid's nightmare, I wondered how any parent could survive it. Sighing in the dark, I thought I was right about my sixth sense, but it was too late to change our destiny.

As soon as the girls woke up, I called Dave, who in Hong Kong was eight hours ahead, 'Honey, did you read the news? We are locked abroad. I'm devastated.'

Dave paused and then reassured me, 'You will be fine. Stay with your family until things become better. The girls will love Spain.'

My body relaxed while I watched the girls explore the corners of our hotel room, giggling. I said goodbye to Dave, went to Alba and Maia, and told them, 'Girls, we are going to start our adventure.'

Maia, who had just turned three in June, looked confused, 'Mommy, what's an avvventure?' she asked, curious. I kissed the little dimple on her right cheek, picked her up and told her we had to change our clothes and discover secret places in the hotel.

I had a thousand questions but I had no choice other than to continue the journey to La Gomera, and so we took the big Fred Olsen ferry and traveled across the deep blue Atlantic Ocean to the small island. At the ferry pier, we jumped in the first taxi that took us from San Sebastian to the valley of Hermigua. My secret master plan was well kept, and as we reached the family house, I opened the green gate and let Alba and Maia walk first to surprise my family one by one. First my mom, then my sister Vicky, Grandma, their cousin Chloé and all the uncles and aunties. I filmed the moment on my phone, and they were all in shock, seeing the little girls they barely recognized. My grandmother was watching the scene from the balcony. I looked up, and she had her hands on her face and was overwhelmed with joy. She looked much older and had turned grey since I had last seen her, two years previously, but her wrinkles couldn't hide her happiness.

'This is a present from life. I have prayed so many nights for this moment,' she cried.

I walked toward her and teased her, 'Grandma, you prayed, but I'm the one who brought them all the way from Hong Kong. Come, give a hug to your favorite granddaughter.'

I sent the video to Dave with a message that read, "You were right. It was worth it. Love you".

It felt right being back to my roots, even though we were locked abroad. As the weeks passed, I woke up every morning hoping to read positive news about the quarantine decreasing in Hong Kong, but it didn't. Instead, things were becoming darker and more sinister. Penny's Bay had reached maximum capacity, and the government was rehabilitating new areas for isolation across the city, and repurposing hotels into quarantine camps. An entire class of an international school in Discovery Bay had been ordered into quarantine, with twenty kids aged eight and nine having to isolate with a parent for three weeks. A young British couple made the international news because they refused to be separated from their infant when the baby tested positive. I could have been that mom, and the thought terrified me.

One evening, I received a message from my friend Esther. It read, 'We are out of here. This place is crazy,' and contained a link.

## THE FLIGHT HOME

I clicked on it and saw a picture of government officials leaving residential buildings carrying big red bags. A batch of hamster pets recently imported to Hong Kong from the Netherlands had been identified as a carrier of a contagious virus variant. The government had ordered the immediate detention and euthanasia of all the little creatures in the contaminated batch, which contained hundreds of them. Public servants dressed with protective suits like astronauts visited flats across town in large groups and left carrying those heavy red bags where they collected dozens of terrified little hamsters who were unaware of their imminent fate. I felt sick seeing the pictures in the newspapers. I thought of our puppy Django back home, the girls playing with him, and the dozens of children who would be heartbroken, knowing that their innocent little furry hamster was taken away in a big red bag. I thought of the parents making up some story about hamster heaven.

There was no hope we would be able to return to Hong Kong in the near future, and as much as I missed Dave and Django, a new question popped into my mind — Did I want to go back? Was that the place I wanted my girls to grow up in? Would the Hong Kong I had loved ever be the same again? Many people, particularly parents, started to be haunted by the same questions, with Facebook posts of entire families leaving Hong Kong inundating my feed. Anyone with a foreign passport was looking at an exit plan, and even local Hong Kongese started to apply for permits to move overseas, to places such as the UK and Canada, to emigrate from their own country.

I accepted the harsh reality that the newspapers would not be publishing the good news we were anticipating anytime soon, so Dave and I decided that the best temporary solution would be for me to stay in the Canary Islands with Alba and Maia until December and then reassess the situation. That gave us four months to let things back home settle. We didn't want to be separated, but it was the only way to protect our family. If things hadn't improved by then, we would travel to Australia to visit his parents.

One morning, Mom walked the girls to school with me. It was only a five-minute walk, and we dropped the girls at the gate. Mom said goodbye with a smile and kept waving as the girls entered the building. 'Life is full of surprises. I never imagined you would ever live in our small village and your girls would ever go to the local school. It's a blessing,' she said.

I nodded and replied, 'It's all a big adventure.'

With that new plan in mind, I shifted my focus to making the most of life in the Canary Islands and getting to know and live in the place I was originally from but knew very little about. I had enrolled the girls in the local public school of Hermigua called Mario Lherme, where they were the first Spanish-Australian-Hong Kongese students ever. I continued working on my logistics business during school hours, started to study Chinese again through Zoom lessons, and spent the afternoons and evenings with my family, who were always around, happy to help and chat provided it was not during siesta time.

Ten years earlier, my mom had opened her restaurant, Telemaco in Hermigua and we were staying in a small flat next to it. It only had one bedroom, and I slept on the couch in the living room, but it was cozy, and the girls' toys all over the floor made it feel like a home away from home. Alba and Maia loved visiting the restaurant and being assigned jobs by my mom, from placing the table mats to organizing the food in the pantry or watering the plants. She occasionally gave them one euro so they would know the meaning of hard work. Alba often left the flat in a rush with a severe expression explaining she had to work in the restaurant, and I wondered what the teachers thought about

# THE FLIGHT HOME

that at school.

After three months in Hermigua, the girls spoke Spanish to each other as no one else around spoke English. Spanish was fast becoming their first language. My friends were surprised to hear that I went from cosmopolitan Hong Kong to tiny rural Hermigua, but it felt effortless for the girls, and I was happy to spend quality time with my family without the rush of the big city. Alba and Maia were happy at school with their new little Spanish friends. They loved all the teachers, except the English teacher, Hernan, who repeated the same English songs again and again with a Spanish accent, like a broken record.

Dave and I talked on the phone as much as we could, but the eight-hour time zone difference made it hard, especially as he often flew around the world. As a cargo pilot, he was working more than ever because the demand for products like gym equipment, books, and furniture skyrocketed during the pandemic, and the planes were full. I missed him the most at night when on the empty couch, I turned off the lights, but we were both grateful our daughters would never end up in locked up in a container and wouldn't have to wear their Hello Kitty masks anymore.

One night as I was tucking the girls in bed, Alba told me, 'Mommy, do you think Daddy can put us in bed and read us a story one day? His tickle attacks are the best.'

I kissed her on the forehead and replied, smiling, 'I think Daddy is keeping all the tickle attacks for when he sees you.'

Maia added, 'Daddy is the best,' and as I was turning the light out, Alba said,

'My family is the best.'

In December 2021, we said goodbye to Hermigua and the family. I gave my grandma a warm hug, not knowing if it would be the last one, and we waved goodbye from the ferry to the place that had become our second home. We flew to Madrid, where we were finally reunited with Dave after almost four months of Daddy on the screen.

When we saw him at the hotel lobby in downtown, Alba and Maia ran toward him, screaming, 'Daddy, Daddy,' and he picked them both up, lifting them in the air. I watched the scene from behind, soaking in the little bits of happiness. It didn't matter where we were. All that mattered was that we were finally together again as a family.

As Dave started to talk to the girls and ask them questions, Maia replied in Spanish. Confused, Dave continued to speak in English, and Maia started giggling as she tried to figure out why her daddy didn't understand her. After four months fully immersed in Spanish culture and language, she had unexpectedly forgotten all her English and was now only speaking Spanish. I was filming their conversation on my iPhone while saying, 'This is lost in translation,' and we all laughed.

I wasn't worried. Children are like little sponges, and she would relearn English in no time, the same way I had to learn French as a child, but that didn't solve the immediate issue. Alba frowned and decided to take the matter into her own hands. 'Daddy, I will translate for you.' At age four, she had already earned her second job. That little episode was more than just a good laugh. Four months was a long holiday in my world, but I realized it was an entire life in the little people's world.

After two days in Madrid, on December 6th, 2021, we took our last selfie in Spain. We were smiling at the camera at Madrid airport, waving our plane tickets from Madrid to Dubai and Dubai to Sydney. Eight tickets, one family, one destination. Once again, we only had a one-way ticket, but it didn't matter because we were together, and ready for a new adventure.

## CHAPTER TWO
*Becoming Véronique – Inclusion*

Where do you come from?

When I meet someone new, this is one of the most common questions that I am often asked. For most people, it's a pretty straightforward question: you talk about where you were born, where you grew up, and you probably have memories of that one place you once called home.

For me, I have always dreaded that question, and it took me many years to be able to find an answer that I was comfortable with. Do you want to know the truth? The truth is, I still haven't found a good answer, but the difference is that now I'm OK with it.

From the age of five, I started moving countries with my family due to my dad's job. Since then, I have lived in nine countries across four continents. By the age of fifteen, I had already lived in four countries and spoke four languages fluently. When I tell strangers my story, they think it's crazy, fascinating, and often both. But to me, it's normal. Living a nomadic life, changing schools, not owning a house, learning a new language ... All of that is what I see as normal because it's the only thing I have ever known.

I was born in 1980 in Tenerife, one of the eight Canary

Islands, part of Spain. It's a remote place in the Atlantic, close to the Moroccan coast in Africa. The Canary Islands are known in Spain as the blessed islands, as the weather is truly blessed; the landscape is quite magical, with volcanic mountains, white and black sand beaches, lush vegetation, as well as deserts, and snow on top of El Teide, the highest peak in Spain.

At the time, my parents were living in La Gomera, a tiny island to the West of Tenerife. The capital of the island, San Sebastian is a small harbour town and the very last piece of land Christopher Columbus set foot on with his crew in 1492, before venturing west to discover the Americas. Perhaps that's why I was born with a spirit of adventure.

Dad was working at the customs office, a government department in charge of inspecting all cargo that arrived on the island by boat and Mom had started studying at university to become a teacher when she got pregnant with me at the age of nineteen. Dad was seventeen years her senior. Big age gaps were common at the time and my grandfather Hernando was twenty-five years older than my grandmother Mari. Men were the family providers and women stayed at home raising the family, so my mom quit university when I was born to be a full-time mother.

On a very hot day in June when my mom was ready for labor, she and my dad took the Fred Olsen ferry from La Gomera to Tenerife, the big island. They headed to the public hospital in Santa Cruz, and a few hours later I was born into this world. I was a dark skin 4 kg baby, and the passing-by nurses and visitors congratulated my parents for having a big healthy boy. My mom thought I was the cutest baby in the world, but she quickly perforated my ears and attached golden, little baby earrings to them, to make sure people stopped calling me a boy.

All my family from Mom's side are from a village in La Gomera called Hermigua that had two thousand inhabitants in its years of greatness, prior to the big rural exodus that decimated the population. Today it has eight hundred inhabitants, many of them German retirees escaping the cold. Although it's a very small village in a valley, it has two Catholic churches to make sure people don't miss church on Sundays.

As far as we can go back in history, all my maternal ancestors are from that tiny little place. My uncle Domingo is a fan of genealogical trees and random facts in general. He spent hours in the local library digging up the local registries and annals, to track back our lineage. After days of research, he shared the disappointing news that all he found was a very big family in a very small island.

I am the first person in our family to marry a foreigner, ever. Of all the nationalities in the world, I married an Australian. The irony is, if I dug a hole in the ground from the place where I was born and it went all the way through the globe, I would almost go straight into my husband's arms, on the other side, in Australia. Opposites attract each other, and although I don't really believe in destiny, I love to believe it was meant to be, as I could not imagine my life without my Aussie partner in crime. Whenever someone says that the world is a small place, I always think of that.

I only have a few blurred memories of living in La Gomera as a child. I remember the beach, the sun, and the hot sand on my feet. I remember my baby sister Vicky crying in her baby bassinet when she was born. I remember the delicious smells of fresh pancakes coming from the kitchen. I remember holding my mom's soft hand while walking on the street. I remember the excitement when the door opened, and Dad was back from work ready to give me a tickle attack. I remember walking a lot because I had to give away my pram at the age of one and a bit when Vicky was born. Maybe that's why I love running today.

That's all I can remember from the first place I lived in, my so-called roots. Mom tells me that I loved going to kindergarten with teacher Teresa and apparently, I learned how to read at the age of four, as I was always trying to decipher signs on the street. Perhaps that's when my passion for writing started …

In 1985, when I was five, we moved to the border between Spain and France, to a small village called Puigcerdà in the Pyrenees mountains. My dad was working as the customs Chief, as at the time, there was no European Union and therefore no free borders between European countries. Therefore dozens of trucks carrying fruit, vegetables, tobacco, and occasionally drugs smuggled in between, were inspected every day by the customs officers. The customs building was an old stone-grey construction. I remember it being huge, but when you are a child, everything looks so much bigger. Dad and all the officers worked downstairs but he had a private corner office that smelled like leather.

There was a long wooden bench on one side of the common area where the officers would inspect all types of imports, and ensure all the documentation had been issued correctly. The flat where we lived was upstairs. The first time we went inside, Vicky and I started running along the long corridor, chasing each other and discovering new rooms. We played with the echo of our voices from one side of the flat to the other, and our sounds were magnified as there was no furniture to block them. Then, when we opened the door to the living room, I saw a hole in one of the walls with burnt logs of wood and ashes.

'Dad, why is there a dirty hole?' I asked. Dad started laughing and, pointing at it said, 'It's a chimney to keep us warm in winter, as it gets very cold here when it snows.'

Looking around and repeating the word chimney, I scratched my head and then asked another question.

## THE FLIGHT HOME

'Dad, what's snow?'

The cool thing about living in a customs house is that we were virtually living in two countries at once. It's not possible to know where exactly one country finishes and another starts. There is no specific point or a line, but at the age of five, I asked my mom every single day.

The Spanish customs house in Puigcerdà was our home, with Guardia Civil officers directing the vehicles in their green uniform, and then around eight hundred meters further along on the same road, right after crossing a little river, there was a sign with the words "Bienvenue en France". Two elegant French Gendarmes in their blue uniform patrolled the French customs building in the little village of Bourg-Madame. The eight hundred meters stretch that separated those two buildings was "no man's land", the in-between, the cross-border. I was fascinated by this in-between place, and would sometimes run along the stretch to see how fast I could run from Spain to France. In the six years we lived there, I calculate I crossed the border around two thousand four hundred times. Soon, I will get to the why.

I have some vague scattered pictures of my first day at kindergarten in Bourg-Madame in September 1985. The sky was deep blue and the air was crisp. Mom and Dad were talking to Madame Duran, the teacher, while I was playing with Vicky and inspecting this new strange place. The kindergarten room had light yellow walls. It was bright and full of toys; little children were busy playing and giggling. I was excited to join them and run in the outside courtyard where children were playing tag.

Dad adjusted his blue and red tie and told me, 'Have fun and make sure you look after your little sister.'

I grabbed Vicky's little hand, held it tight, and told her we would be OK. As Mom and Dad waved goodbye exiting the room, Madame Duran held my hand and said something to me that I did not understand. Her calm smile comforted me though, and I felt safe holding her hand while I watched my parents walk away and disappear.

She took Vicky to another classroom where her teacher was waiting for her, and we were separated. She then gently guided me to a group of little girls and boys sitting on the floor, playing. Excited, I joined them and listened, but I suddenly became very confused. They were speaking, laughing, and doing the same things all five-year-olds do, but I did not understand a word of what they were saying because they were speaking in French. The feeling was alienating and scary, I wanted to join and play but I didn't know how. I wanted to ask Madame Duran where my mom was, but she wouldn't understand me and I started biting my nails.

It was the first time ever I found myself in a situation where I couldn't understand absolutely anything of what people around me were saying. I couldn't tell anyone that I was hungry and a bit scared because everything was new. I was just looking around trying to read facial expressions and body language, trying to make some sense of the brouhaha around me.

Surprisingly, I have mostly sweet memories of those days. I think there is a universal language that all children, from any background, culture, and language understand: the language of play. Children have a natural sense of fun and fairness, and they also learn how to fight, chase each other, and play games without having to speak any specific language. Madame Duran was kind and taught us kindness. Sometimes I think that everything I needed to learn in life, I learned at kindergarten.

However, at times I was overwhelmed by being constantly surrounded by foreign words the entire day, and I always felt like an outsider because all the other children were from the other side of the border. I needed to find my own way to fit in, and I

## THE FLIGHT HOME

found my answer in puzzles. The classroom had lots and lots of puzzles of princesses, animals, and vehicles, and depending on the level of difficulty, once we completed them as a reward we were given different stickers and stamps. I loved all of them and cherished my collection of stickers. Above all, I loved the moment when Madame Duran gave me the stickers in front of everyone and said, 'Bravo' to the clapping of the other children.

One day, I went to Madame Duran after I completed the hardest puzzle for the eighth time. She smiled and told me, 'I can't give you any more stickers for doing the same puzzles again and again. You are too smart. How about you play outside until we receive new puzzles?'

The new puzzles never came, but those words had more impact on me than she ever knew. It gave me the confidence to go outside; outside the classroom to play with the other children, outside my world of puzzles, outside my comfort zone. That's how I learned to speak French.

Most children had a best friend in class, someone they always sat together with and held hands with when they had to queue up to go to the bathroom. I didn't have a best friend because I think all were taken, but I figured if I learned how to speak like them, maybe I could have a best friend too. My parents say I learned to speak French in three months. I don't have a specific recollection, but I remember making my very first friend, Laure, and from the moment we became best friends, we were inseparable. How it happened was quite random, we were both born one day apart in June, and the teacher told us we would celebrate our birthday together on the same day in class. It made perfect sense to the logic of two five-year-olds that we became best friends; our birthdays were so close together. That created an immediate bond between us.

I asked her, in French, 'Do you want to be my best friend?'

When she said, 'Yes' the world smiled at me. Five days later, the school term ended for the summer holiday, and just like that, I finished kindergarten in France with my very own best friend. I guess I must have stolen someone else's best friend, but I felt I deserved it.

Moving into primary school in 1986 was a big deal. My parents let me choose my first school backpack, and after browsing and touching every single one at the store, I picked a Hello Kitty bag. On the first day of school, when the bell rang, I entered the classroom holding Laure's hand. It was the first year of primary school and we would learn how to read and write. We were the big kids now.

All the students were assigned their individual desk for the year. Mine was an old wooden desk with a round hole at the far-right side. We all thought it was funny and started giggling, pointing at all the holes. The teacher, Madame Comas explained to us that the hole was used many years ago when the students wrote with fountain pens. The little bag containing the ink was placed and fixed inside that hole and then replaced again and again with new ink. The students would dip the pen tip into the container which would magically suck the ink until it had enough. They would repeat the movement dozens of times a day. I looked around all the desks trying to find the one that had a hole in the left. I checked each and every one of the little desks but quickly realized there was no desk for me, as they all had the hole on the right-hand side. It was also my first realization that I was left-handed, and just a little bit different from all the other children.

I imagined how difficult it would be to write on that desk if I had to use my left hand, moving across the desk to the right every single time I had to refill the ink. It must have been hard for those left-handed children back in the day. My desk had some stains of dark blue ink from side to side that could not be removed. I concluded it must have belonged to some left-handed student who, just like me, didn't have a suitable desk and it made me feel a little special.

I was relieved that we didn't use those ink holes anymore. Because it was a public school, they probably hadn't received funds to replace those desks with new modern ones. So, the hole was there for the naughty kids like Pascal and Rémi, who intentionally dropped pens and paper balls through them, and for me as a reminder of how lucky I was to be able to write with a normal pen. I was also told by my friend's grandma that being left-handed was seen as something really bad when she was a child and that some teachers used to fold the left hand of those naughty left-handed little children behind their backs, to force them to use their right hand to write and become normal. The thought terrified me. I even did a trial using my right hand to see if I could be normal like the other children, but the result was an utter disaster. I couldn't be fixed.

When we started to learn how to write, Madame Comas would ask each student to go to the blackboard and write some words with a stick of white chalk. I was nervous and excited when she called my name for the first time, and I went to the blackboard and started my task. As I meticulously wrote, I heard some whispering and laughing behind my back. I turned around and some boys were pointing at me laughing because apparently, I had a funny way of holding the chalk. I had never noticed how a left-handed person writes but that day I discovered it looks awkward and amusing because we roll our hand in a funny way to go from left to right. Clearly, writing must have been invented by a right-handed person.

At that moment, I felt my cheeks burning and I was relieved I didn't have to face the classroom. I just wanted to disappear but there I was, standing in front of the whole class with nowhere to hide. I think Madame Comas saw it in my eyes.

With her calm voice, she addressed all the students, 'Most people in the world are right-handed but only a small number are left-handed. Veronica is very lucky to be left-handed because they are very special and smart people.'

Those words touched my heart. I grabbed the chalk again and continued writing on the blackboard with a smile. I believe my passion for writing started then, in that little classroom with Madame Comas, just because she told me I was special, and I believed her. I also think it's no coincidence I have very neat and curated handwriting. It was my way of saying that different is beautiful too. Madame Comas was my very first mentor in life.

My second year at school was a walk in the park. I spoke French with a thick southern French accent just like the other French children. I had my best friend, I knew all the school songs, and even changed my name to Véronique, the French version of Veronica. I can't remember who, when, or how it was changed, but I remember loving having a French name like the other French children. It made me feel I belonged.

I always had great marks and school was a happy place. I even had my very first boyfriend at the age of seven. He was a French boy with dark hair and cute dimples. One day, Nicolas told Olivier, who told Virginia, who told Laure who told me that Nicolas liked me. I immediately blushed. The next day, I told Laure, who told Virginia who told Olivier who told Nicolas that I liked him too. We never held hands and barely talked to each other, but it was a good feeling to be liked.

Going into year four, we were all excited and nervous to meet Madame Combescure. She was a new teacher at school, which was quite rare as most teachers were from Bourg-Madame and had lived there their entire life. We didn't know what to expect and when the school bell rang, we ran into the classroom. I could hear my heart beating with excitement. I wanted to meet my new teacher, study hard, and be liked by her.

By then we were allowed to pick our own seat for the year, so I picked mine, in the middle of the classroom, close to Laure and as far away from Nicolas as I could manage, even though he was still my boyfriend.

Madame Combescure said, 'Bonjour,' stood up in front of us, and started to call out the students' names from a sheet she was holding. As usual, we would formally say, 'Present,' and stand up straight in military style. Because my family name starts with the letter L, for Llorca, I was always in the middle of the list. I was ready when she called out my name loudly, 'Véronique Llorca Mendoza'. I stood up and said, 'Present,' with a smile. She paused and inspected me from head to toe. The silence lasted for ages until she finally said, while adjusting her thick glasses, 'Mendoza, Hmm … Spanish? That's an interesting name. I'd better put you in front of the classroom. I like to keep the naughty ones close to me.'

I sat down and looked at the floor. I was wearing a pair of new pink ballerina shoes I had kept in my closet like a treasure to wear on the first day of school. I took a deep breath trying to keep the tears inside my eyes, and kept on staring down wondering what I had done wrong. I was the only one among the twenty children who had to move seats. I gently closed my new pencil case and packed my backpack. I didn't zip it because I didn't want to make any noise, and I moved to the front of the class where I sat in front of Madame, avoiding any eye contact. Although I had changed my name and I spoke French just like the other children, she reminded me I was different.

Being different meant I would have to work extra hard to be able to blend in and be accepted by my teacher. My face was burning, as I felt all the little French eyes staring at the Spanish girl. This time though, no one laughed. Whether they were terrified by the new educator, or out of respect for me, I never knew, but the only noise I could hear was the little voice inside me telling me not to cry. I didn't.

Mom picked me up after school. When we were in the car, she asked me, jokingly, 'So, how was the first day? I'm sure your new teacher loved your shoes!'

I paused and replied, 'It was a great day Mom,' and quickly changed topics to avoid more questions.

During one of the school breaks that year, a very annoying boy called Emmanuel started to call me all sorts of nasty names. He would say that my skin was dirty because I was darker than the other children and call me Spanish tiger, dragging other boys into it. Sometimes there were four of them calling me names. If it was OK for the teacher to pick on me, then it was certainly fine for the other children to do the same. By then, I wasn't having any of it, and I fought back every time and called him all sorts of terrible names too.

One day, during the break, Emmanuel pulled my long dark ponytail from behind, dragging me backward. I turned around and gave him the biggest punch in the face and he started bleeding from the nose. I didn't plan to hurt him, but I didn't want to get hurt either.

Madame Combescure saw his bleeding nose and said, 'Mademoiselle Llorca, go to the Principal immediately,' without asking what had happened.

Going to the Principal's office was the worst nightmare of any kid at school. Rumour had it that when a student was sent to Monsieur Margouet's office as punishment, he would give them a smack straight away before asking why they had been sent there. There was no presumption of innocence.

## THE FLIGHT HOME

I had never been to his office except once with my parents when they enrolled me in primary school a few years earlier, and I was certainly hoping never to go again. Once a little boy called Rémi was expelled from his classroom and sent to the Principal's office because he had misbehaved. I can't recall exactly what Rémi did, but he was so terrified by the thought of meeting the Principal, that he actually fainted on his way before making it to the office. Today was my turn.

Mr. Margouet was an imposing man with a black greyish beard. We were all intimidated when we saw him patrolling the corridors. Some children would find a corner to hide in, others would sprint to the courtyard outside even if it was snowing, or squeeze behind the curtains. I had always liked him though. He seemed tough but kind, and after having been in the school for a few years, I wasn't scared of him anymore, although I still found him intimidating.

That day, I knocked at his wooden door knowing what was coming next, and ready to get my smack, even if I was just trying to protect myself.

When he asked me to come in, I said, 'Bonjour' as I awaited my punishment.

As I opened the door, he lifted his eyes and looked at me frowning. He left the newspapers he was reading on his desk. It was Le Monde. Suddenly, everything was happening in slow motion.

He touched his grey beard and said, 'Bonjour Mademoiselle Llorca. I have to say, I'm really surprised to see you here. I was not expecting you. What happened?'

He knew the story and background of each of the children at school because it was a small school and because he cared. He knew my story, he knew my grades, he knew me. I explained my crime while feeling the sweat on my hands. I didn't cry or stutter.

I stood tall and looked him straight in the eyes. 'Monsieur, Emmanuel has been annoying me and calling me nasty names for a long time and today he pulled my hair from behind. I turned around to protect myself, I punched him and ...'

He interrupted me before I could finish my defence argument. 'Well done Miss Llorca, you are a tough young lady. But next time, please don't punch anyone. Just come to me first, OK? Now go back to your classroom and let's pretend this never happened.'

I said 'Merci, Monsieur Margouet,' and left the office with a smile that screamed victory.

I don't know what happened to Emmanuel, but I suspect Mr. Margouet must have talked to him as well, as he never bullied me after that episode. Or maybe he realized he couldn't bully someone who was going to stand up to him. In any case, I didn't have to worry about that boy anymore.

That year I went the extra mile to study and get the best grades in my class. If my handwriting was neat and my grades were perfect, then Madame would not have any reason to pick on me. She might pick on someone else, but I really didn't want it to be me. Throughout the year, my efforts paid off and I received the highest grades in all the subjects, even French. I did all my homework alone without any help because Mom and Dad didn't speak French.

I vividly remember often receiving the best score in the entire class because Madame made sure the experience was memorable for everyone, as she had a nasty way of announcing the results. On the day of the test results, she called out the names of all the children, from lowest to highest score, asking them to stand up and go to her desk. She then handed them their notebook back with a few comments. The ritual started with a very long list of nasty comments to the poor-scoring students, and she would finish it, usually praising the top three students, sometimes none.

## THE FLIGHT HOME

Needless to say, how unimaginable this practice would be in any school system today, or so I hope, but back in the 1980s in the public French school, it was the norm with Madame. There was always anticipation and anxiety before the public announcement of the grades. During the humiliation session, Madame would very often call first either Emmanuel or Carlos, a Spanish boy who was older than the rest of us, because he had repeated a class. She would refer to them using insults and sometimes throw their notebook in the air at the same time, making the scene more Dantean, as the children had to kneel on the floor to pick up their notebook and their pride. She had a whole repertoire of nasty names, but she had two favorite French expressions that are actually quite funny, although not in that context.

'You are as dumb as a donkey,' or, 'You write like a cat.'

I don't know what it is with French people and their colloquial expressions, but I have never seen a cat writing and I would question whether a donkey or any animal is actually dumb. I felt sorry for Carlos because he was a nice boy, and he was Spanish like me, so we had something big in common: we were different. As for Emmanuel, I agreed that he was dumb, not because of his grades but because he thought there were tigers in Spain.

That's how I remember having great grades. I don't actually recall anything about the grades or the content of the exams, but I remember being called last and being praised by Madame; reluctantly, I imagine, because she had no other option, since I had scored the highest grade. I had figured out the loophole in her bullying system, and I had finally won the battle or at least a battle.

Sometime throughout the year, she started to like me, as she realized I was disciplined, obedient, and wouldn't give her any problems. Instead, she must have assumed that good students could help her to influence the naughty ones. So, one day, she said that she was going to make naughty Emmanuel change seats to be next to someone who would make him "less of a donkey". Of course she picked me, so there I was again, haunted by Emmanuel who was haunted by Madame.

Of all the homework I received throughout my entire five years of primary school, I only recall one piece. Madame gave each student a book to take home to practice reading and then in turns, read it out loud in class. Back at home, I started reading the chapter assigned for that week but also the one after, as I wanted to be ahead. When I was reading the first paragraph of that chapter, my heart suddenly sank. It read, "The trains in Spain are filthy".

I was eight and I felt embarrassed and ashamed of what my eyes were reading. I felt sick thinking that in the coming days, someone in class would have to read those words out loud and everyone would be looking at me, the Spanish girl, and at Carlos. I had nightmares about trains that week. Finally, the day of the torture arrived. We were in reading class, and every student was assigned one paragraph to read out loud, one after the other, following the seating arrangement. I knew what was coming, and I just wanted it to happen quickly, and move on to the next paragraph.

When it was time to read the mortifying paragraph about the trains, she paused. She adjusted her glasses as she always did when she was brewing nastiness inside her head and then with a hint of a smile, looked at me from the corner of her eyes.

'For this part, I would like to invite Véronique to read.'

My turn wasn't due until five paragraphs later but there I was, in front of everyone, reading out loud and clear with a very dry throat, 'The trains in Spain are filthy.'

As expected, all the children laughed. All except for Carlos. Thinking back at that episode, still very vivid in my mind, I recall the famous sentence by Angela Markelou. "People will forget what you said, people will forget what you did, but people will never forget how you made them feel".

I never forgot what Madame did, and I never forgot what she said, although in my case, I had to say it myself. I never forgot how I felt either, and in fact, when I shared this anecdote with my husband thirty years later, I couldn't help the tears falling down my cheeks.

Bullying is very lonely and can come in many different shades of grey. But bullying from the teachers and educators, those who teach our children and help build a better world, is unforgivable. I don't know what the title of that book was that held these cruel words. I even Googled it to see if I could find it, but I couldn't. No child deserves to read that sentence and feel lesser than the rest.

The following year, my sister Vicky who was just a year behind at school was assigned Madame Combescure as her teacher. I had already warned her about the French witch but at the same time, I was hoping that because I had good grades, my little sister would not have to go through the same purgatory.

At the end of the first day of school, I entered the car with Mom to go back home in the afternoon. I couldn't wait to hear about Vicky's day, and as she entered the car, a few minutes after me, I asked her, 'So, how was the witch?'

Vicky started laughing and said that Madame's first words were, "Hmm…Llorca Mendoza. I know that family name. I hope you are as smart as your sister Véronique, or else I will be disappointed".

I really did not see that coming, but I realized that a bully will always be a bully. Months later, my sister had to read the sentence about the filthy trains in Spain.

The rest of the years in the French-Spanish bubble were

full of happiness and that carefree feeling only children seem to have. We used to ski every weekend in winter in the many resorts around the mountain like Font-Romeu, Puigmal, and La Molina, and make snowmen in the garden with real carrots, black buttons, and hats. We also had two red sleighs that Dad helped us pull up in the fields across from our house, which were covered in beautiful white snow.

Around that time, I also learned a new language: the language of sports. Mom and Dad took me to the ice-skating rink in Puigcerdà, rented some blue plastic ice-skating boots for me, and let me go by myself. From the first moment, I felt like there was something natural about sliding on the ice. I fell multiple times on the ice-cold floor, and in spite of my wet butt, I got up every single time with a smile, until I was finally able to stand and slide across from one side of the rink to the other. It felt like magic.

When I finished, I put the boots away and I told Mom and Dad, 'I loved it! Can you please sign me up for figure skating lessons? I'm going to ask Santa for a pair of ice-skating boots for Christmas.'

My parents bought me my first pair of figure ice skates that same year and I treasured them like gold. They were white, very rigid at first, and delicately crafted in leather. Nothing like those horrible and uncomfortable plastic ones I had tried the first time. They enrolled me into classes with a big group of girls, all locals from Puigcerdà. There was only one boy called Albert. I loved it from day one: the discipline, the feeling of flying in the air, the glittering outfits, the competitions ... It was my passion, and I couldn't get enough. I trained daily, sometimes before school, when it was still dark and cold outside. Sometimes I trained after school, eating my afternoon snack in the car on the way to the ice rink.

The only thing I did not like about figure skating was that

## THE FLIGHT HOME

the girls spoke a different language that was neither French nor Spanish but a mixture: Catalan. It is the language spoken in Barcelona, Girona, and the Catalonia region in Spain. In small villages, like mine, it was the main language at school too, with Spanish taught as a second language. Although I was quickly able to understand everything, I would always answer back in Spanish, so I was given the nickname Canarian, as I came from the Canary Islands.

Being left-handed in the ice rink was a big handicap, as when we were all skating backward to gain speed for the jumps, we would skate in opposite directions, so I either had to zig-zag through the busy traffic, wait until everyone was done, or have the coach Mayte pause the entire session to let me take my turn. I ended up making great friends, but we still accidentally bumped into each other anyway skating backward with both skaters collapsing and ending up on the ice.

Once I heard two older girls whisper in Catalan, thinking I didn't understand, 'She's so annoying, always skating in the wrong direction.'

One day, the municipality of Puigcerdà organized a special festival to celebrate the Day of Catalonia, and the President of the Region, Jordi Pujol was invited as a guest of honor, together with his wife, for the opening ceremony in the ice rink. The coach wanted to prepare a three-minute choreography with a boy and a girl dressed in the traditional Catalan outfit as a tribute. The choice was extremely easy — Albert was the only boy, and because he was left-handed, he would have to be paired with a left-handed girl, so it was the first and last time in my life that being left-handed gave me an advantage.

We both entered the ice rink holding hands, did our performance, and grabbed a bouquet of red and yellow flowers, the colors of the Catalan flag. We then made our way through the public, walking up the stairs of the stadium under the sound of the claps until we reached the important guests and gave them the bouquets and a kiss for the picture. The next day, I appeared in the newspapers with the President, and everyone thought I was a lovely Catalonian girl.

Besides having their own language, many Catalans also claimed an independent Catalonia, free from Spain. The sentiment was particularly strong in small villages, as they were more isolated, and the Catalan culture was deeply rooted. People were proud of their language and they would look at my dad with disdain when he addressed them in Spanish. The TV programs were different from the ones in Spain and the news only talked about Barcelona. The food was different too, with a lot of red meat and *pan amb tomaca* which was a baguette with olive oil, grated tomato, and juicy Spanish ham on top.

Of course, I didn't know any of this at the time, however, one night in the middle of winter in 1990, Mom and Dad rushed into our bedroom to wake us up and dress us quickly in whatever warm clothes they had found. In a matter of minutes, we were out of the house and into our car half-asleep, leaving everything behind. It was pitch dark outside, we drove to the Park Hotel, a few kilometers away, and the owners, who were our friends, let us stay for the night.

Later in life, I found out the truth. There had been an anonymous bomb threat call made to our home in the middle of the night. Spanish government agencies such as customs and police stations were frequent targets for separatist groups and those types of threatening calls were frequent in the 1980s when the independentist movement ETA was on fire. Fearing the worst, my parents didn't sleep that night, but Vicky and I thought it was a great adventure, especially because we missed school the next day and played hide-and-seek along the corridors of the hotel.

## THE FLIGHT HOME

We went home later that day, and everything looked the same; it was all a false alarm.

The best time of the year was the days leading to Christmas, when the grass fields were covered in white snow, the lake was totally frozen, and the skies were blue without a single cloud. Puigcerdà looked just like a perfect winter postcard. When we weren't outside building snowmen, or doing snow angels, Dad used to light up the fire in the chimney at home and we loved sitting in front of it, watching the flames dance and the fire consuming the old Spanish newspapers and wooden logs.

Mom would always cook the most amazing food and we were a happy little family. My mom is the type of woman who became a second mom for all my friends. She welcomed everyone, inviting my friends to stay over for the weekend, and cooking delicious Spanish meals that everyone loved, particularly paella, the typical Spanish yellow rice with seafood. Marion, one of my friends from school, would come to our home after dinner to eat with us a second time because apparently, she didn't really like her mom's food and so for years, we had a fifth plate on the table at dinnertime every evening. To this day, at least three of my girlfriends call her "our Spanish mom".

Dad was busy at work and therefore we saw less of him, but because his office was just downstairs, I would often sneak in to say, 'Hi,' at noon, showing him my school report or just pretend to be a spy, hidden behind a column. I loved smelling his cologne as I approached his office because it meant he was there. He was never too busy for me and my sister and always made a point of leaving his office to give us a hug, even if it was just for a few minutes. These minutes meant the world to me. He taught me how to ride a bike, how to arm-wrestle, and how to be on time.

He taught me how to play chess with a beautiful chess set, made of solid iron pieces on a black and beige marble table. It's the most beautiful chess set I have ever seen. We spent hours playing and we pretended we were competing in different leagues: the local league, the regional league, and the international league. The games could last for hours until we would reach the final checkmate point, and most of the time he won. I had a tantrum the first couple of times but in spite of those, he never let me win. When I did, it was as a result of my own skills and virtue. He sometimes gave me hints when I was about to make a false move, but he thought that teaching me how to lose was a far more important lesson, than teaching me how to win.

One afternoon, we were about to play, and he was just finishing reading an article in the newspaper. He was talking to Mom about it and I overheard the word "polyglot".

'Dad, what's a po-ly-glot? I asked, emphasizing every syllable.

'It's someone very smart who can speak five languages.' It turns out it is someone who can speak several languages, as 'poly' means various in Greek, not necessarily five, but that's what he told me.

I loved the weird sound of that new word I had just learned, and before we started playing the game, I said, 'Dad, one day I will be a polyglot.' We both smiled and entered the European League of chess ...

One day, in 1991 after we came back from school, Dad and Mom told Vicky and me they had some news. We all sat around the dining table, and Dad announced with an excited tone, 'We are going to move to another country in a few months. It will be like an adventure and you will have a new bedroom and many new toys.'

We were both shocked by this sudden news, and Vicky immediately started crying. I sat quietly and asked, 'But, Dad, when are we going to come back home?'

We had been living in the in-between for six years and I had never thought of living outside our bubble. I thought children were supposed to live in their bubble until they became grown-ups, who then built a different bubble.

Dad looked at Mom, who was comforting Vicky in her arms and he went on, 'We are not coming back here. We are going to have a new home and you will have a new school and will make new friends.'

I remembered the first day at kindergarten. Would it be the same?

I then continued the interrogation, 'But why do we have to move? Why do we have to leave our home, our school and our friends?'

Dad always talked to us like adults, with no sugar-coating, plain matter-of-fact talk, so he patiently explained about the European Commission (predecessor of the European Union), and the Treaty of Maastricht of 1991. He explained that this meant the border separating Spain from France had to be closed, and the trucks could now freely go back and forth without him and the officers having to inspect the cargo inside. The beautiful grey-stone building had to shut down forever and he was given a new job in another country. It was my first lesson in politics, at the age of ten and I'm happy it came from Dad. The next obvious question was … moving where?

## CHAPTER THREE
### *The Color of Your Skin Matters – Justice*

When I heard Brazil was our next destination, I started to repeat the word in my head with different tones, to try to process it and see what it sounded like. I felt a world of mixed emotions, from sadness to excitement, anxiety, curiosity, and everything in between. At ten, I had the intellectual capability to understand what moving to a new country meant. I knew it was the biggest country in South America and the only one where they spoke Portuguese, not Spanish, because it had been colonized by the Portuguese. I was able to check where it was on the map and guided by my index finger, virtually travel from my little village in the Pyrenees all the way to Rio de Janeiro. It was a long way away, and it also meant going from the northern hemisphere to the southern one. I had already studied the hemispheres and the line of the equator at school, and I also looked up Brazil in Dad's treasured hardcover encyclopedia collection. I discovered the Brazilian flag and loved the colorful green, yellow and blue pattern with its twenty-six stars, each representing a different state.

We took off to Rio de Janeiro on the evening of October 30$^{th}$, 1991. Dad had left a few weeks earlier, to find a flat and start working before Mom, Vicky and I arrived. The Iberia Barcelona-

## THE FLIGHT HOME

Rio de Janeiro flight with a stopover in Madrid was the longest flight I had ever taken in my life, and I loved it. The big Airbus was like a space rocket, and I, the explorer, was taking off to a different planet. Long-distance hauls were very rare in those days, and I felt like a super lucky little girl to be able to fly around the world. I was sad about leaving my friends behind but equally excited about the adventure that was coming ahead. I discovered then I had a spirit of adventure, and the unknown was thrilling.

Since I was a baby, I had never been a big sleeper, and the excitement of the flight and the new life were keeping me awake during the flight. I wanted to absorb every detail, understand the buttons and inspect the elegant outfits of the flight attendants, who kept passing by with drinks, snacks, and treats for the children. We were sitting in business class, which was an absolute luxury, and the plane was rather empty.

A very nice male flight attendant kept on passing through my corridor with drinks, and sometimes he was empty-handed. He had the most charming smile and kept on staring at me every time he passed. He was Brazilian and said, 'Oi,' which means 'Hi' in Portuguese. I knew because Mom had organized some Portuguese classes for us in Puigcerdà with a lovely Brazilian lady called Mara. She was the first contact I ever had with Brazil and I remember her feminine voice, her long dark hair, and her home which smelled like Brazil to me.

I was happy to have an adult pay me attention and wanted to be polite, so I kept on smiling back. Mom and Vicky were sleeping, snuggling together. A woollen blue blanket with the Iberia logo covered my legs as I was wearing black shorts and the air-conditioning made me cold.

At some point, I saw the flight attendant waving in my direction. He was standing just next to the galley, on the corridor, and he was by himself. He was pointing toward his legs, making a gesture for me to remove the blanket and shift my body to the side. I was confused and didn't know what he wanted me to do, so I removed my blanket, put my Barbie doll on the side and moved to the side, toward the aisle with my legs uncovered. He was staring at my legs but I didn't understand why. He gave me the thumbs-up and I felt pleased to pass the test. He did it multiple times throughout the flight, always looking around nervously as if he was hiding something. I thought it was fun, like a secret game. At some point he made a gesture asking me to go toward him. Mom was still sleeping and suddenly to me everything felt off, and creepy. I remembered Mom and Dad telling me to be careful with strangers and my intuition told me he was one of them, even though he was smiling, and was supposed to look after me.

I was eleven, I was a child, and at that moment, I realized that the man with the charming smile and the elegant uniform, didn't see me as one. I had never kissed a boy, and when I understood what was happening, I started to feel sick and ashamed.

Mom was still sleeping, so I walked to the back of the plane, as far as I could go from the flight attendant, and locked myself in the economy-class bathroom. I started sobbing, lifted the toilet cover, and started throwing up, but nothing came out other than bile and shame. I looked in the mirror and splashed water over my face. I felt dirty and naked, all I could see was the man's smile trying to see my body. I pulled myself together, went back to my seat, and decided to stay still, pretending I was sleeping, for the rest of the flight hiding under the blanket. I didn't sleep for one minute. My hands were sweating and I was frightened by a smile that still haunts me to this day. Leaving the plane was a relief, when the flight attendants were standing at the door to wave goodbye, I avoided all eye contact and never saw him again. Somewhere between the old continent and the new one, an eleven-year-old girl had her innocence stolen in the sky.

When we landed at Galeão Airport in Rio de Janeiro, I took the courage to tell Mom what had happened as we were waiting in the luggage carousel. She looked shocked and confused as if she had never considered that I could be anything other than a little girl playing with Barbies. She was trying to hide her tears but I could see the little veins in her eyes turning red.

She hugged me, and whispered, 'I'm so sick I don't know what to say. I'm so sorry I didn't notice anything. I should have been there to protect you. I'm so sorry.' She looked around making sure no one was listening.

I took her hand and that comforted me. Suddenly everything felt like a blur. Maybe it was all the vivid imagination of a little girl full of fantasy? Maybe it was all my fault? I was lost in my thoughts when Mom continued with a serious tone, 'Please don't tell your dad. I don't know what he's capable of doing if he finds out but he would lose his temper, and I'm worried he might do something violent. He would take justice into his own hands.'

I knew exactly what Mom meant. Dad's temper was as strong as his values. My pinkie promise to Mom was to not say anything, and I never broke it. Dad was on the other side of the airport gate, waiting for us in the arrivals lounge, with a big smile and a bouquet of red flowers for Mom. Vicky and I rushed toward him, and he lifted both of us in the air.

'Daddy, Daddy! We missed you!' we cried.

He smelled like his usual cologne, exactly the same way he did in his corner office and I was happy to be a little girl again. He introduced us to Armando, the official driver who would drive us home.

The very first thing I noticed going outside was the smell. I have always had a very developed sense of smell and tend to associate smells with places, people, and moments in life. It didn't smell bad, but it was different. It was a mix of humidity, tropical fruits, and rain. If I close my eyes and think of Rio now, I can still smell it.

Dad was now a diplomat for the Spanish Government in Rio de Janeiro and that was the first time I heard about consulates. On the drive to our new home, I had a hundred questions but didn't have time to process the answers because of what was going on outside our car and inside my busy little brain.

I looked through the very dark windows of the car and told Dad, 'These car windows are so funny, they are really dark and people can't see us from the outside.'

Dad was sitting in the front seat, next to Armando. He looked at me through the front mirror and explained, 'They are called armored windows. They are common in Brazil. Many people have them for security, to have protection while driving.'

I pressed the button in an attempt to open the window but it was locked. Armando noticed what I was trying to do and nervously said, mixing Spanish and Portuguese, 'We never open the windows when we drive in Rio. It's just to keep you safe.'

I didn't say anything. I was feeling tired and leaned my head against Mom's shoulder, wondering whom we needed protection from and why and then I snoozed. When I opened my eyes, we were still driving. Outside, everything looked different—noisy, busy, and chaotic. Coming from my small village, Rio felt like pure chaos with cars honking, beggars selling all sorts of stuff at the traffic lights, and lots of people everywhere.

I was fascinated by the people around me and was mesmerized by the diversity of races, ethnicities, and fashion styles. There were black people, mixed people called Mulattos, Latinos, and a few blonds as well. I discovered that there was also a small number of Caboclos amongst the Brazilian population. They are a mix between Indigenous Brazilians from the Amazon and

## THE FLIGHT HOME

European descent. It was astonishing how different people from the same country could look, and up to today, Brazil remains the most multicultural country I have ever visited, among over 50. The Brazilian passport is the most expensive in the grey market of counterfeited passports in the entire world. The reason for that is because anyone, no matter the color of their hair or their skin, could pretend to be Brazilian. I found this out later because Dad dealt with frequent passport thefts at the consulate.

'Look, Vicky!' I shouted when we stopped at a red light, pointing outside.

A group of barefoot children who looked around seven years old started to walk around the cars. Some had torn old T-shirts and were selling cigarettes and candies, others were improvising a quick and unsolicited car clean with a sponge. People inside the cars had their windows shut and looked away pretending the children didn't exist. Vicky looked confused too.

I asked Mom, 'Why aren't these kids at school?'

Mom looked at the children with pity and told us, 'Not everyone is lucky enough to go to school. In Brazil, some children start working very early, on the streets, to earn money.'

I remembered all the times I complained about not wanting to go to school in the morning. I had never thought of it as being lucky until I saw those children who looked skinny and dirty, begging for money on the streets. I never complained again about going to school.

After an hour-and-a-half of hectic driving, we finally made it to the side of Rio I had seen in movies and magazines. First, the famous Copacabana Beach with its golden beach and coconut trees, then we moved on to the iconic Ipanema Beach, famous for the global musical hit *Garota de Ipanema*, or *Girl from Ipanema*. October was the beginning of the rainy season in Rio, and everything looked grey. It wasn't the sunny welcome we expected from the Hello from Rio postcards, and I have bittersweet memories of that first day.

After we had passed Ipanema, Dad told us we were going to enter our new neighborhood, called Leblon. I immediately liked the name; it sounded French and therefore familiar. The car finally stopped on Sambaiba Street 666, in the *condominio* (compound) called Quintas e Quintais. It was a huge compound made of multiple buildings with shared facilities, tennis courts, and swimming pools; however, the first thing I noticed were the various policemen at the entrance gate. They were all black and carried visible guns while patrolling the entering vehicles.

Dad must have seen the concern in our eyes, and casually added, 'Don't worry, they are not policemen. They are security guards to make sure people don't rob the flats.'

Vicky looked at me terrified, and I whispered, 'Don't worry, we will hide our toys so that the robbers can't find them.'

We started laughing and finally, the car came to a stop. We were about to discover what home looked like.

Our new home didn't feel or smell like home at all. It was on the fourth floor and had a large terrace facing the jungle.

As Dad opened the door, he said, 'Surprise!' He pointed in excitement toward an adult-size pool table in the middle of the living room, occupying half of the room. Mom, Vicky, and I pretended to love it but deep down I could tell we were horrified at having that gigantic green rectangle blocking the way. Mom looked shocked and I could tell she had no idea what to think.

The flat was already fully furnished and the decoration was tacky and dated. The walls were painted beige and it looked like an older person's place. I then entered a bedroom and it felt like intruding into someone else's life.

'This is your bedroom, do you like it?' Dad asked, proud of his decoration.

## THE FLIGHT HOME

I looked around, inspecting the empty shelves, the carpet, the girly blanket with pink and white stripes, and tried my best to put on a smile.

Before I had a chance to say anything, Dad added, 'Your toys will arrive soon in a container with all our things. It will be just like your old bedroom.'

I opened one of the cabinets and it was empty. I sat on the bed and lifted the blanket. It smelled new, just like this new life that had my name on it. I looked to the side of the apartment and saw that my bedroom had a sliding glass door that led to the terrace.

'Vicky, let's check out the terrace!' She joined me and we both started to explore. We saw a beige nylon hammock hanging from the ceiling. After some awkward attempts, we both made it inside and started giggling.

'Can I tell you a secret? I don't like it here,' I said.

'Me neither,' added Vicky, bursting into a big laughter.

We both started laughing, trapped in that hammock.

I heard a noise on the side and whispered, 'Shhh ... look, it's a cute little monkey.'

The tiny monkey had a very long brown tail and had jumped from the jungle straight into our terrace, only a few meters away from us. I had only seen monkeys at the zoo and smiled at the idea of having a monkey as a pet. I couldn't wait to write a letter to my best friend Laure and start telling her about my adventures. Even though I had been in Rio for less than 24 hours, I already missed her. Dad joined us on the terrace and said these monkeys were called *macacos* and were very friendly and curious.

While Mom and Dad were busy talking adult stuff, Vicky and I continued our mission and we kept on opening new doors and exploring corners of our new life. As we entered the kitchen, we saw a door at the back. We opened it and found a tiny bedroom and a small bathroom. We were curious about who this child's size room was for. In the meantime, we thought it would make a great room for our toys, except they hadn't arrived.

The first day in our new home felt lonely and grey, just like the street. It was grey outside and empty inside. Nothing was familiar and it was difficult to suddenly call a new place home. We were tired and jetlagged. It was raining heavily outside and there was nowhere for us to go. We tried to turn the TV on, but all the channels were in Portuguese, and although Portuguese and Spanish are similar languages, they were different enough for us to lose interest in the cartoons. Dad had gone out shortly after we arrived to sort out paperwork, and Mom, Vicky, and I were lost without a sense of direction, in a home that didn't feel like home. What were we supposed to do when we moved to a new country? Is there a manual for day one? I had no idea and was trying to compose my own manual without much success.

Out of the blue, Vicky looked at Mom, and without saying a word, she burst into tears. It was an unexpected and suffocating cry, as if she had been holding it until she could no longer keep it inside. And the more she tried to hold it in, the more it escalated. Mom tried to comfort her at first, giving her a cuddle, and without any warning, Mom started sobbing too. Seeing my mom cry for the first time was one of the most baffling moments in my life as a child. I was standing there trying to comfort my mom who was trying to comfort my sister in a circle of tears.

Suddenly, I had an idea: I took off my pink T-shirt and my black shorts and climbed on top of the pool table from one of the sides. I stood tall on the green surface, with only my panties on, and started to improvise a silly dance. Mom and Vicky stared at me puzzled, trying to figure out what the heck I was doing up there, but it became obvious I was impersonating the chicken dance with the Spanish lyrics and a lot of passion.

There I was at eleven years old, figuring out life and writing page one of my manual for moving to a new country. I feel really embarrassed telling this story to the world but was compelled to share it because it's the first happy memory I have of the four years we lived in Brazil and because it made Mom and Vicky laugh. And we laughed really hard until we had tears again, this time of joy. When I see a pool table these days, it reminds me of the story of the chicken dance. In the end, it was a good thing Dad made that random purchase and luckily, I never had to dance on top of it again ...

We wouldn't start school until the beginning of the new term, in February 1992, and during the weekdays, Mom would often take us to Dad's office in a modern building in the city center called Rio Sul, in the district of Botafogo, just past Copacabana. It was the tallest building we had ever been in. The bottom floors were a shopping center, and the top floors were dedicated to office space.

We used to hang out in the mall for a couple of hours and then took the lift upstairs to visit Dad in his office on the 16th floor. My first time in the office lift was quite an experience. An impeccably dressed black woman was seated in a small chair facing the lift buttons. She greeted the customers with a smile and pressed the buttons of the floors as requested by the passengers. That was her job, hours and hours of vertical traveling, going up and down.

In my child's mind, there were a lot of useless jobs in Rio, as in jobs that were not needed, and this looked like one of them. Plus children love to press buttons and are happy to do it for free. Who created the lift job? The lift ladies were lovely, and over time they came to know us by our names.

The Consulate of Spain in Rio was impressive. Dad's office had some amazing views facing the city and every little detail was curated: the leather couches, the green plants at the entrance, the fine leather furniture. It smelled like a consulate. Vicky and

I quickly learned everyone's name, from the Brazilian secretary who helped the guests check in at reception, the Spanish officers, and the Consul General, Gonzalo, who was also a very elegant man, just like his very elegant office. Everyone was nice to us there.

My favorite member of staff was the security guard called Denzelton. He was a big black guy with a contagious laugh and a permanent, mostly toothless smile. He always wore his grey uniform and had a gun or two in his belt, just like the security guards in our building. He lived in a *favela* called Rocinha. *Favelas* are ghetto neighborhoods with a very high poverty index and crime. We had been warned against *favelas* and the people living there from day one. They were dark places with dangerous people to be avoided at all costs. Back then, some *favelas* were even out of scope of the federal police's jurisdiction.

*Favelas* were a parallel reality, like a Matrix world ruled by the drug dealers called *narcotraficantes* and the mafias, governed by their own unwritten laws. There were often clashes between the internal gangs but the police mostly kept out of it, and let the gangs take care of establishing the order, very often with a lot of blood spilled from both sides. I never went to any *favela* during my four years in Rio, although we drove past some on our way to school. Even though they were just a few kilometers away, I saw them every day on the news. I'm sure there were other super-cool dudes like Denzelton, but I never had the chance to meet any of them. He joked with us and had an easy-going vibe. He was like the good cop in a Hollywood movie.

When it was time to start school in February 1992, my parents picked the French school, called Lycée Français. There are Lycées all around the world, mostly in big capital cities with large French expat communities. They are usually named after famous French poets, writers or scientists, and ours was called Lycée Molière, honoring the late French author. The curriculum was taught in French and that was a relief because by then French had become my first language, and Vicky and I spoke French to each other, especially when we didn't want Dad to understand.

The school was on the other side of the city, in a residential colonial neighborhood called Laranjeiras, with plenty of trees and greenery. Mom drove us to school every day, from Leblon, passing through Ipanema, Copacabana, and then venturing into the commercial neighborhoods of the city. It took around one and a half hours each way depending on the traffic, and it was pure chaos: traffic jams, people honking and swearing, accidents every other day, children asking for money, and cars ignoring the traffic lights. After a few months, we stopped noticing all of that.

Rio has the best traffic jams in the world. Sometimes, they were so bad, especially on the weekends, getting in and out of the city, that people would just step out of the car and start dancing Samba on the street or flirting through the windows with the people in the cars around. I hated that long commute, but it became part of the routine, and then I forgot that I hated it. That's the good thing about routines.

On the first day of school, I went in excited, as I was ready to make new friends after three long months. On arrival, as it was after the long summer break, all the children hugged each other and shared stories in Portuguese. No one noticed me and I felt invisible. I pulled an empty notebook from my backpack to keep my hands occupied. I looked at my purple Casio watch hoping the minutes would pass faster, and when the bell finally rang, I walked toward my classroom in relief.

The head teacher was Madame Lorenzana, a tall slim red-haired woman who looked very serious with her hair up in a meticulous long ponytail and brown glasses. She had a deep voice and introduced me to the other students but no one was paying much attention, so she started the class.

My first year at school was lonely and I spent many breaks alone, reading, or pretending to do the homework I had already done at home, to look busy. I was eleven and it was a difficult age to make new friends. An undefined age where I was neither a child, nor a teenager, and I was going through a lot of changes, physically and emotionally. The circles of friends were already sealed, and I didn't belong to any. I was shy as I am an introvert by nature, and struggled to reach out to new people. I realized I needed them but no one really needed me and I hated the awkwardness of taking the first step. To make things worse, even though the main language in the classroom was French, in the corridors and outside everyone spoke Portuguese.

There were mostly two groups of students: children of French expats who were in Rio for a short period of time and only spoke French, and the children born and raised in Rio, often to a French dad and a Brazilian mom, who spoke French as a second language. I didn't fit into any of these two groups, but I learned Portuguese quickly, so that gave me a better chance at making friends.

My favorite times of school were the lessons because it was the only time when I was able to be included and feel valued. I spoke better French than most other children, who had only learned it at school or through one of their parents, as a second language.

Madame Lorenzana was very serious and formal and spoke French with a very refined accent. She always called us using our family name. One day, she asked me to read one paragraph. I started, and as I pronounced the word *pomme* (apple), she abruptly stopped me. 'Your French is excellent but your accent is terrible. The accent from the south of France is tacky. We have to fix it this year.'

## THE FLIGHT HOME

Like many countries, France has many different accents depending on the region, and some accents are seen as more refined than others. I did indeed have an accent from the south, as I learned French in the south, and that's the only French I had ever heard until then, and now I was being told I sounded too southern and tacky. I didn't make a big deal out of it though. I just recall her big mouth wide open articulating the word *pomme* multiple times with big gestures imitating my accent, and it didn't suit her at all. She was an elegant woman from Paris with an elegant French accent. After that day, I repeated the word *pomme* and all the other words in my head over and over again, sometimes in front of the mirror, and over time, I learned how to sound just like her.

If I spoke French on the phone to anyone today, they could probably think I'm an elegant French woman, with an elegant French accent. They could even believe I am Madame Lorenzana herself. I had learned how to blend in and become a new me, a better me that would be accepted. I had been fixed.

In her defence, Madame Lorenzana was not a bully, unlike my previous Madame. In the *pomme* episode, some students started laughing at me, and she stopped them straight away and scolded them with her elegant French accent.

'I'm not sure what you are laughing at. Her French is much better than yours and she is not even French.'

She had the deeply ingrained belief that having a so-called polished accent would give anyone a better chance at succeeding in life, and just like that, she projected her own bias onto me. I consider myself to have done pretty well in my professional life, however, I suspect it had nothing to do with having an elegant French accent.

As the months passed by, I was trying to figure out where my place was in this new world. It took me several months to make new friends and I often begged Mom to send me back to boarding school in Bourg-Madame.

Every time Dad came back from work, I would rush to him, 'Dad, Dad, are there any letters from Bourg-Madame?'

Once a month the diplomatic courier arrived and it would often contain dozens of letters from our friends back in France. I kept every single one of them as a reminder that I did have friends.

During that long year, I had to make a huge effort to overcome the barriers of being an introverted girl who felt different and came from a different place. I made efforts to listen to the same Brazilian music, wear the same clothes, and speak the same way, with the same *carioca*, Rio accent. I also convinced my parents to let me go to the evening birthday parties of the other children and they reluctantly agreed to most.

Toward the end of the year, I made my first friend, Sabrina, a French-Brazilian girl who looked similar to me. She had long dark hair and dark skin. I helped her with homework she hadn't had time to prepare. When the results came out, she received a great mark and she came to say thanks.

During the break, I took the courage to ask her, 'Do you want to come to my place this weekend?'

She said, 'Yes,' and she said, 'Yes,' again twenty-two years later, when I asked her to walk behind me as my bridesmaid, on my wedding day.

Through Sabrina, I discovered another side of Rio I fell in love with. She was extroverted, loud, and fun, and her horoscope was Cancer, just like me. We couldn't be more different but we just clicked. Once I had my first friend, it was easier to make new friends, and a few months later, I had my own circle of friends and Rio became my favorite place on Earth. I decided I wanted to look and speak just like a Brazilian. I left the Barbies behind

## THE FLIGHT HOME

because we were now grown-ups.

My group of French-Brazilian friends became my circle of trust. We spent hours and hours chatting at school and on the phone, the old-school home-line phones where you had to dial the numbers by pressing the buttons with your fingers and you had to say, 'Hello,' to the parents on the other side of the line, before talking to your friend. I remember once spending two hours talking to Sabrina on the phone during the weekend. One day, our moms had a parent-to-parent conversation and concluded it would be more efficient to organize sleepovers than having the phone lines saturated, arguments with teenagers about phone usage, and expensive phone bills. From then onwards, Sabrina started to come to my place for entire weekends. We were happy, the phone bills became cheaper, and our parents stopped complaining.

I also became friends with Rachel, who went to the Lycée and lived in Leblon, not far from me. She was Brazilian, French, and Greek. We both started rollerblading around the same time and we would meet up on the weekend to rollerblade for hours along Vieira Souto, the big avenue along Ipanema that was closed to traffic on Sundays.

Going to school, I asked Mom to drop me as far from the gate as she possibly could so that the other teenagers wouldn't see that I was being dropped off by a parent. I think all the other teenagers did the same, and we all pretended to have mysteriously rocked up at school, fully ignoring the existence of our parents. We were grown-ups.

One evening, Mom and Dad said they were going out to a consulate function, and they told us we would have a babysitter to look after us.

'Mom, a babysitter? That's ridiculous. I'm twelve years old. That's so embarrassing, I don't need anyone to look after me. We didn't even have a babysitter in Puigcerdà and I was ten!'

I was fuming. Dad then announced that the babysitter was going to be Denzelton, from the consulate, and Vicky and I immediately changed our minds and loved the idea. He was such a cool dude, and he didn't talk to us like children, so we approved of him.

That night, Mom and Dad were getting ready when the security guard downstairs called to announce that Denzelton had arrived. Dad gave the green light for him to come upstairs and I overheard the security guard saying he was taking the back lift.

'Dad, why can't Denzelton use the front lift like us?' Dad shrugged uncomfortably, and sighed, 'That's the way things are here. Some people use the front lift and some use the back lift. I don't like it either.'

'I don't like to make people go to the back. It's really a silly rule made by silly adults,' I said.

The bell rang and Denzelton came in. In Brazil, all wealthy residential buildings have two lifts, the main lift takes you directly to the main door and is usually nicely decorated with a mirror and some golden decoration, and the back lift, grey, and dull, often smells like trash. The main lift is used by the owners and their guests, while the back lift is used by the domestic helpers, the security guards, and anyone else who doesn't fit into the first group. Children on the other hand are smarter and use whatever lift arrives first as they don't care about mirrors and gold.

Denzelton came in and we were over the moon to welcome our personal superhero bodyguard to spend the evening with us and tell us cool stories about the *favela*. Mom and Dad left and we barely noticed it. Denzelton must have come directly from the office, as he was wearing his usual uniform and even had the guns with him.

## THE FLIGHT HOME

'Denzelton, do you think I can hold your gun just to feel it?' I asked.

He started laughing and said, 'No way. If you touch this gun, we are both in serious trouble. How about you teach me how to play pool instead?'

And that's the story of how Denzelton, a guy from the Rocinha, learned to play pool with a Spanish girl who wanted to get rid of the back lifts.

One year later, in 1993, Dad had to organize a social function for the consulate, and he was in charge of selecting the venue. It was fun to accompany him on the weekends, as we visited several clubs in the city, and they were all nice and fancy. After doing the tour of the venues, Dad settled for one. It was the Yacht Club. The main building was white and elegant, with a dark blue flag on the roof that moved with the wind. The pier was located a few meters away and dozens of boats and yachts were docked along it. I had never seen so many boats together.

I asked Dad, 'Who do all these boats belong to?' pointing at a white yacht on the right.

'They belong to rich people who are members of the club,' Dad replied, following my finger.

'They look so beautiful! Do you think we can buy our own boat?'

'If you want to have a boat, you will have to work for it and earn your own money. I will give you all the tools and will teach you how, but you have to put in the effort yourself,' he answered.

I paused to reflect on what he was saying, and suddenly connected the dots, 'Just like when we play chess, right?' Dad grinned.

A few days later, he called the club to confirm the details of the function. The staff had asked him to disclose the details of the consulate staff that would be supporting the event, Dad provided the names of guests and they said everything was fine, but they would have to find another security guard as Denzelton was not suitable. Dad was telling the story during dinner and I couldn't hide my disappointment.

'What's wrong with Denzelton?' I asked.

'There's nothing wrong with him. These idiots are the ones who need fixing. I'm not having any of it. Just because of the color of his skin.'

I immediately understood what he meant, and put my fork down. I lost my appetite thinking of my hero from the *favela* and how the color of his skin mattered.

I looked up at Dad and said, 'I think I don't want to buy a fancy boat or join a fancy club anymore, and by the way, you always tell us not to swear.'

One person who played a big role in my years in Brazil was Nolita, an old black lady who was hired to clean and cook at home under the title of *empregada*, which meant, maid. It was the norm in Brazil and still is for upper middle-class families to have at least one *empregada* working and living at home. That's why most flats have a small living area behind the kitchen. Nolita spoke slowly, walked slowly, and did everything slowly, but she had the kindest smile and would always be nice and gentle. She was like a grandmother to us, because outside of Mom and Dad, she was the closest figure to a grandma we had, and because she looked like one, although I never knew her age. She also came from a *favela* and went back there on the weekends to see her family.

Mom and Dad offered her to come and work at home during the day and go back to her place in the evening but she said she preferred to stay in her little room with her privacy rather than take multiple public buses every day, at the risk of being assaulted or suffering the frequent public transport strikes. I loved Nolita. Her food was terrible and salty, but she spoiled us and was always in a good mood. When I did something naughty, she smiled and promised she wouldn't tell my dad. We were not used to having someone else living with us but Nolita quickly became a part of the family, a Brazilian grandmother with a kind smile, a contagious laughter and a big heart.

On the first day she started working at home, we were all getting ready to eat the meal she had prepared for lunch; it was white rice with *feijao*, a black bean that is the Brazilian national dish, as it is cheap and filling. Dad asked her to sit down with us and eat together. She looked at him really confused, as if she hadn't understood my dad's broken Portuguese.

She blushed and apologized, 'Sorry, Sir, I have a lot of work to do in the kitchen. I will eat later by myself,' before awkwardly disappearing behind the kitchen door.

We later found out that in Brazil, the domestic helper would never sit down with the employers to eat together. She had never done that before and was determined not to start now. Dad didn't insist. Later that evening, when I went to take the plates to the kitchen, I saw Nolita eating her dinner by herself. I noticed she didn't know how to handle the knife and fork properly and I understood the real reason why she didn't want to eat with us. She had never learned how to use the cutlery properly and was embarrassed to eat in front of us.

Nolita was always joyful and cheerful, singing Brazilian *Bossa-nova* songs while slowly performing the house chores, and she was always respectful of Mom and Dad. She called them *A Senhora*, which means, madam, and *O Senhor*, meaning sir. This is the polite way of saying "you" in Portuguese. English is a very democratic and inclusive language because there is only one word for you. While this seems obvious to English speakers, in all the other languages I have learned, there are two different types of you: the colloquial and informal way, and the polite way that is used to show respect and formality. We use the normal you for friends, family, and people we are close with and the formal you for older people, teachers, bosses, clients, or at interviews. I prefer to only have one you and not have to worry about reading people and their social status or age to accurately pick the appropriate you, as I always end up offending someone if I use the wrong one. My least favorite word in English though is the word "Ma'am" because although it's meant to show respect if I am called this it makes me feel like a dinosaur, and since I turned forty I hear it more and more.

After three years of living in Rio, it had become home and I loved every bit of it. I embraced the beach, the music culture, the street language, the never-ending TV shows called *Novelas*, and everything that had Brazil stamped in it. Weekends were the best. With my girlfriends, I visited Ipanema Beach, but not just any spot on the beach. All the cool people went to the beach in front of the lifesaving guards' Post 9, even if that meant that your *canga* or beach sarong would be overlapping with the neighbor's, creating a colorful pattern across kilometers of golden sand. No one ever carried towels to the beach because it was considered not cool.

Rio girls brought cute Balinese-style sarongs that would often be sensually wrapped around their hips, and the guys did not carry any towel at all because it was not deemed masculine. Very often they didn't wear flip-flops either. Guys were tough and they would either stand tall with their arms crossed showing off their muscular pectorals, or sit on the burning sand hoping some girl would invite them to sit on her *canga*. Post 9 was the best. Everyone knew everyone and we could spend hours there, gossiping, tanning, swimming in the cold Atlantic water, and checking the boys out. There is an entire underground beach culture in Rio, and I learned the ins-and-outs of it, just like the locals.

First, we didn't go to the beach on Sundays, only on Saturdays. Sunday was a busy day where every single person from the suburbs headed to the beach, so it was considered dangerous and messy. Looking from the hills, it was extremely crowded, and it was impossible to see the white sand underneath the thousands of people. Sunday was the beach day for the people from the *favela* and we were warned not to go, so we never did.

Second, we didn't go to any random spot on the beach, it was always the same place where we would meet the same people. There was a post for teenagers (Post 9), a post for hippies (Post 10), a post for older people with children (Post 11), and a post for the residents of the *favela*. I don't know who wrote that rule, but everybody knew it and followed it religiously. There was also an unspoken code for the surfers, specifying where each gang sat and surfed but because I was not into surfing, I didn't bother to learn that code. Whenever someone intruded into a post where they were not supposed to be, no one said anything, but it became very obvious, and every single person would spot the stranger in a heartbeat. There was no masking there. The only people who were totally oblivious to this rule were the many American and European tourists, with their flower shirts, their sandals covering their white socks and their Fujitsu cameras strapped around one shoulder. And Dad. He would occasionally show up to pick me up with his Hawaiian shirt but I was always fast enough to spot him before the crowd and run toward him before he would mortify me in front of my cool crowd.

One day, Dad and I had agreed that we would meet on Ipanema Beach at 11:00 a.m., just next to Post 9. I was just a few meters away from the post, lying on my *canga* talking to my friend Rachel. By 11:15 a.m., there was no news of Dad, which was suspicious as he was always on time. All of a sudden, a whole brigade of policemen arrived and started to patrol the beach frantically and everyone started to gather around to see what the fuss was about. I was curious as well but when I looked closer, I was horrified to see Dad in the middle of the brigade. The policemen were calling my name on the speakers. I was embarrassed and pretended I didn't hear it. He was on time but hadn't spotted me on the beach and assumed I had been kidnapped by some *favela* gangs, so the consulate had issued the red alarm because the daughter of the Vice-Consul was missing. There were six fully armed policemen looking for me following my dad's orders, and there I was, horrified in front of my cool gang trying to dig a deep hole in the sand and magically disappear.

By the time I turned thirteen, in 1993, I had found my identity in Brazil, and when people assumed I was from Rio because of my thick *carioca* accent, I didn't deny it. I was proud to be one more ordinary person blending into the crowd. I learned the lyrics of popular songs, wore cool fashion brands like Cantao and Salinas bikinis, and hung out with my little group from the Lycée. Rio was vibrant, colorful and there was always something on: a concert on the beach, a party at someone's house, a BBQ ... I couldn't think of a better way to live through adolescence although, for Mom and Dad, these were the most stressful days of their lives. Dad was particularly paranoid about violence and kidnapping and was the strictest dad of all dads in the entire world but I was smart at finding tricks and shortcuts to get to where I wanted to be.

On the 3rd of December 1993, the news broke that two little French boys were kidnapped on their way to school, a few yards away from their parents' house. Their school was my school, the Lycée Molière. I didn't know them because they were eight and

## THE FLIGHT HOME

ten and I was thirteen. Their dad was the managing director of an important multinational IT security firm. When the teachers announced the sad news during the class, we all felt shocked, saddened, and devastated because it was our school, our people, and our world, and that day, someone broke a little piece of it.

For a moment, I imagined the title of the article could have been about two little Spanish girls aged twelve and thirteen and the idea really frightened me, but as a teenager, I thought that those things only happen to other people or on TV. We never found out what happened behind the scenes, whether there was a ransom paid or a negotiation between the government and the kidnappers, supposedly *favela* leaders, but a couple of days later, the little boys were released safe and sound, and we all moved on.

A few months later, another incident happened at school. We were in math class when suddenly we all heard noises from outside. It sounded like scattered fireworks. The teacher, Mr. Colette put the chalk back on his desk and asked us to stay quiet.

Minutes later, the school alarm went off and we started to hear other teachers yelling, 'Shooting! Shooting! To the floor! Now!'

The students around me quickly jumped from their desks and lay down on the floor, face down. I followed and heard giggles around.

'Yeah, shooting day means we all get to go home early!' said Pedro.

It was my first time experiencing a live shooting. There was a *favela* not far from the school up in the hills of Laranjeiras, and the conflict between the local gangs had escalated into an open gun shooting. The police arrived shortly after and the parents were asked to collect the children immediately. The next day we all went back and acted as if nothing had happened because shootings were part of life in Rio.

Because I lived in so many different countries, one of the questions I'm asked the most is, 'What was your favorite country to live in?'

This is a very hard question to answer because when I was growing up, my filters, taste, and the things that mattered, changed over time. Violence was certainly part of Rio, but sadly, because it was a part of our everyday life, it just blended into our routine. Except for the kidnapped boys and the shooting at school, what I saw was mostly on TV, so there was an element of distance.

Most of my friends were robbed at some point throughout the years, especially when they were without their guards, but I knew what areas to avoid, and definitely did not use public transport of any kind. Vicky was also robbed once by two teenagers, on her way back from the beach. She was only carrying some cash and they took the money and the apple pie she had just bought at McDonald's. She told me the story at home and she was really upset about the apple pie. We both started laughing. I believe we also had luck on our side and didn't end up at the wrong place at the wrong time.

Looking back through my teenage lens, Rio was the best place to live in the entire world and I made the best friends there. Thirty years later, I invited four of them to be my bridesmaids: Sabrina, Rachel, Marion, and Stephanie, and a few other friends from Rio came to my wedding, even though they had to travel around the world to be in Ibiza with us. I still carry a little Brazilian flag in my heart with many stars; my friends.

I am often asked if I am Brazilian, especially by Brazilians. Recently, in the lift at the Gold Coast University Hospital in Australia, a medicine student asked me in Portuguese,

'Brazilian? Can't deny when you see one, right?'

The lift door opened and I replied, 'Right,' because I wasn't

## THE FLIGHT HOME

going to tell her the story of my life, and because, deep down, there is still a little Brazilian in me.

In 1995, the four years of Dad's appointment in the consulate were coming to an end, and I was in pure denial about leaving. I was loving everything Rio had to offer and couldn't imagine living anywhere else. In April, Dad announced that he had been assigned his next destination by the Spanish Government and once again, we had a few months to plan our departure. I had zero expectations or excitement because the idea of living somewhere else was inconceivable, so when he announced the Netherlands, I didn't have much of a reaction. I think he could have named any country in the world and I would have reacted the same way, with the typical indifference teenagers are known for. Even after discovering my future country, I was more focused on living my Brazilian life until the very last day.

That last day is when reality hit me like a truck. It was July 1995 and we drove to the airport in the consular car, one last time, passing through the very city that had become home. When we arrived in this country, it was grey and dark, but this day was sunny and colorful. It might have been just a coincidence, or perhaps a reminder that places are just places and it's what we make of them that matters. I was silent in the car and could feel the tears rolling down my cheek. Saying goodbye to Leblon, Ipanema, Copacabana, the French Lycée, and the Cristo Redentor, the symbol of the city … It was like playing a movie from the end backwards and ending it at the first scene, where it had all started.

Brazilian Portuguese is one of my favorite languages because it's playful, colorful and has so many expressions, nuances, and different ways of describing the same thing. Languages tell a lot about a culture and its people, and Portuguese reflects its people; it's witty, funny, street-smart and it has a soul too. My favorite word is *saudade*. I have never found a good translation in another language. It's the feeling of missing someone or something. It's close to nostalgia but it's a different word, and a great word with a lot of depth.

At the airport, we were getting ready to go through the boarding gate, and all of a sudden, we heard our names, 'Veronica! Vicky!'

We looked around and saw two, four, ten, and then twenty friends. I don't know how many there were in total, but the whole airport seemed to be filled with our friends from school. They had come all the way just for us and had prepared a surprise farewell with signs and handwritten letters. We all started crying and laughing and crying and laughing again, and that's how I said goodbye to the city that adopted me as its own. There was *saudade* all over my face and my heart.

# Chapter Four
## From the Bathroom to the Stage – Self-love

The first thing my friend Marion said when I broke the news that my family was moving to the Netherlands was, 'Amsterdam, you lucky thing! That sounds so cool, I will definitely visit you!'

I pictured us dancing to the beep of the music in some fancy club. Amsterdam sounded like a dream for any teenager. The underground clubbing culture, the rave parties, the Dutch coffee shops with legalized drugs on sale, mushroom cakes, and open sexuality.

Although I was initially underwhelmed by the idea of moving to the Netherlands, the more I talked about it with my friends, the more I started to have a sense of excitement and curiosity. I loved Rio with all my heart but I knew it was time to start writing the very first page of a brand-new chapter in my life.

In September 1995, Dad was appointed as Vice-Consul at the Spanish consulate in Amsterdam. As usual, he was only given two months' notice and he and Mom went first to sort out everything. Finding a school, renting a flat, signing all the paperwork and a million other administrative tasks. Mom did most of it by herself, without speaking Dutch or even English and I don't think I ever said "thank you" to her.

Vicky and I were staying at my uncle Paco's in Madrid for two weeks while we were in this limbo between countries, once again in the in-between. It was the school summer break in Europe, and we would be flying to Amsterdam in time to start the new school term and a new life in September.

We took the KLM flight from Madrid to Amsterdam and Mom and Dad were waiting excitedly for us at the arrivals gate at the enormous Schiphol Airport. We all had a big family hug, just like we had done four years earlier when we had landed in Rio.

I couldn't wait to hear about everything and I asked Mom, 'So, how is it here, are we going to live in a house in Amsterdam or a flat? Have you visited the French Lycée? When are we starting school?'

We were walking through the airport toward the car parking and I was looking around, trying to understand the signs in Dutch.

Mom was walking behind Dad and she announced, 'The plans have changed. We are not going to live in Amsterdam. There is no French school here so we had to find a different city so you can both study in French.'

I looked at Vicky who was just next to me and she looked as confused as I was. I thought Amsterdam was the only place we could possibly live in the Netherlands. I only knew two other cities I had previously studied at school.

'Rotterdam? The Hague? Where?' I asked, pulling Mom's arm impatiently.

We entered the car, it was a metallic blue Chrysler minivan and this time there was no driver from the consulate. The first thing I noticed is that it didn't have armored windows. The digital clock indicated 2:00 p.m. and I calculated the time difference with Rio. My friends were six hours behind and were getting ready to go to school now.

'Alkmaar', said Mom. 'We are going to live in Alkmaar.'

## THE FLIGHT HOME

I had checked maps from Holland multiple times but that city didn't ring a bell. 'What? Where is Alkmaar and what's in Alkmaar?' I asked curiously.

Mom looked back at me from the front seat. She was trying to look excited.

'It's a small town in the north and has the most famous cheese market in the country. There's a lake in the middle of the city that freezes in winter and becomes an ice-skating rink so you can figure skate again!'

'Mom, you know I hate cheese and I haven't ice-skated in years!'

Vicky started laughing and said, 'Well, I do love cheese.'

I looked through the window as we were driving along the highway toward Alkmaar. I wanted to tell my friends I lived in the coolest city in Europe and write them a letter about coffee shops and marihuana. Instead, I would have to tell them about the different types of cheese.

'So when are we starting school at the French Lycée in Alkmaar?'

Mom stared at Dad who was concentrating on driving.

'Well,' she replied, 'there's no Lycée there, it's called the European School. It's the only school where you can study in French. The only thing is that you also have other languages as part of the program.' I was expecting to hear Spanish and English when Mom went on, 'You will learn English, German, and Italian.'

'Mom,' I yelled, 'that's crazy. I don't speak any of those languages. I have the baccalaureate exam in two years. How am I going to learn three languages at the same time?' Dad was driving and started giggling.

He looked at me from the front mirror and said, 'You always wanted to be a polyglot, don't complain.'

Mom explained that the European Schools were a group of schools created for the children of European Commission's officers ... The very first European School was established in Brussels and then spread across Europe, to all the cities with European public servants. In the case of the Netherlands, there was a nuclear power station run by the European Commission in the city of Petten, fifteen minutes away from Alkmaar and that's the reason they had created a small European School there, our new school.

I wasn't sure how I was going to learn three languages on top of the very demanding curriculum of high school but I had no say in the decision. There was no Internet then, so one of my very first purchases was three pocket-size dictionaries of English, German, and Italian; I would carry them everywhere. The other purchase was a warm pair of pink gloves.

Just like the first day on arrival in Rio, the Netherlands was all a blur. Coming from Rio, with its exuberant nature, hills, beaches, and chaos, the Netherlands felt quiet, monotonous, and flat. We could be in the car for hours, and would accidentally drive into the neighboring country, Belgium, without realizing it, as it would look and feel the same, no mountains, no hills, and millions of blond people riding bikes.

When we saw the sign for Alkmaar, Dad took the exit from the highway. He started driving around a lake and I noticed that all the houses looked exactly the same, just like the Dutch houses seen in postcards. It was like a perfect little town with perfect triangle-shaped red roofs, little green backyards and long glass see-through windows. Even though it was still 3:00 p.m., the streets were empty except for a couple of neighbors walking their dog and taking the trash out.

'Dad, all the houses look the same here, they are identical, and there are no people on the street, how boring.'

## THE FLIGHT HOME

Dad replied, 'Welcome to socialism. Don't complain, we could have ended up in a communist country.' I immediately thought of China and felt relieved to be in Holland.

We finally made it to our new home, a cozy duplex identical to the next cozy duplex. The house was mostly empty except for a dining table in the living room, a TV, and some cushions on the floor.

I looked around and asked Dad with a cheeky tone in my voice, 'No pool table this time, Dad?'

He started laughing and replied, 'You are giving me ideas. Home sweet home.'

Even though it was still the end of summer, the weather was cold and it was raining. Nothing reminded me of Rio, and this place was grey. Everything was grey, the sky, the houses, the roads and so was my heart. I was looking around trying to find comfort between those four walls but all I could see was a home that didn't feel mine.

I went upstairs, opened the door to my new bedroom, and told myself, 'Home sweet home.'

The next morning, I woke at 5.00 a.m. It was dark outside and I was anxious to start my first day at school. I remembered all my other first days in Bourg-Madame and Rio and had no idea what to expect. I went through my clothes and tried on different things. Eventually, I decided on a pair of light blue Levi jeans and black Nike sneakers that were fashionable back in Rio. I looked in the long Ikea mirror wondering if it was the right look.

In the morning, Mom drove us to school and dropped Vicky and me at the front gate, wishing us luck. The European School was a mixed bag of everything. It was a very small school, with only a few hundred students and small classes, my French class had only five students attending. The Finnish class only had one student, Essi, because her dad worked at the Petten station, and therefore they had to offer a Finnish stream, even if she was the only student in the class. The Dutch stream was by far the largest and most popular, so speaking Dutch would certainly have been an advantage to making new friends but I didn't speak any of it. I spent most of the first day by myself trying to find my way around different classes, corridors, the language, and figuring out where I had to go every time the bell rang. The first week went by and I had barely talked to anyone other than the teachers.

I was busy learning English, German, and Italian on top of the regular subjects in French. Outside the main Dutch group, the rest of the school was like the Tower of Babel where everyone spoke a different language and came from a different place. During the school break, I heard people speaking in English, Finnish, Arabic, Italian, German, and other languages I couldn't understand.

The first two months went by quickly as I was always busy buying things for our new home, helping Mom run errands, and doing all my homework in four different languages.

One evening after school, we were having dinner together and Mom said, 'How about you invite some friends over this weekend? You can organize a sleepover, just like in Rio.'

I put the fork down and replied, 'This is not just like Rio. I have too much homework and anyway, I have no friends here.'

Mom tried to comfort me, 'You just need to give it some time. You are new here but you are smart and fun. You just have to put in a bit of effort.'

I bit my lip and replied, 'You don't get it. We were living in Rio and now we live in the middle of nowhere. I have no friends because no one likes me here. I'm done, I have to finish my homework.' I pushed my chair out and went to my room.

When it was bedtime, I went to see Mom in her bedroom and said, 'Sorry Mom, I really miss Rio and my friends. Everything is

## THE FLIGHT HOME

so different here. People at school are really weird.'

Mom replied, 'I miss Rio too but we are here now so let's make the most of it. I'm sure there are some nice people here too.'

It was early December 1995. Winter was approaching and the harsh weather made everything harder, especially as my friends in Rio were getting ready for the tropical summer. Our furniture still hadn't arrived from Brazil, as container ships were always delayed, so we only had the bare minimum at home.

I had brought with me a photo album with pictures from Rio that my girlfriends had given me as a farewell gift and every night I would flick through the pictures before going to bed. In the evening, Vicky and I watched TV on the floor, sitting on some Ikea cushions next to the heater. The movies were all Hollywood hits in English. I still didn't speak English well and the Dutch subtitles made it even more confusing but it was the only fun thing to do. I watched MTV as well, wondering if my friends in Rio listened to the same hits. It was too cold to go outside and the shops closed early, so we couldn't go shopping either. The home cinema sessions became the highlights of my days and that's how I started to learn English, on the floor of a home that didn't feel like home, eating popcorn to bring some sweetness to my sour heart.

One day, during the school break, I was having a snack by myself, a pitta bread sandwich with ham and cheese. It was the same one Mom made in Rio most days but it tasted different here. It took me back to Rio, bringing back memories from the Lycée when suddenly I heard, 'Veronica, right?'

It was Dounia, a Moroccan girl from my French classroom, dressed in a long black coat. I smiled and nodded.

'Do you want to sit with us?'

I joined Dounia at her table where she introduced me to some other students I had seen around the school. I don't remember what we talked about but it was the first time I was invited to join someone else's table.

The cold was becoming unbearable. Alkmaar is close to the North Sea and the wind coming from the north was arctic. One morning, when we were rushing toward the car on our way to school, Vicky looked at me and started laughing as if I was the biggest joke.

She pointed straight into my eyes and said in between giggles, 'You have frost in your eyelashes, it's so ridiculous!' I was very self-conscious and immediately touched my eyes. I felt the frost and we both started laughing at my ridiculous white eyelashes.

The days were getting shorter and the temperature kept on dropping. We never saw the sun anymore during the day. It was dark when Mom dropped us at school at 8:00 a.m., and dark when she picked us up at 3:30 p.m. I missed the sun, my skin missed the sun but my heart missed it the most.

Every day, on our way to school there was a giant thermometer displayed on the road from Alkmaar to Bergen, that indicated the temperature in degrees Celsius. Every morning the bets were on and whoever got closest to the score won. When the temperature dropped below zero, we started to worry: -1°C, -2°C, -3°C. It couldn't go much lower, or could it? We were so cold that we made Mom promise that if one day the temperature hit -10°C, she would turn around with the car, drive back and let us stay at home. Mom was always very supportive of our studies and would never let us skip class. She probably thought the temperature would never go that low, but one morning, when we reached the thermometer, there it was: -10°C.

Vicky and I yelled at the same time, 'Mom! -10°C! You promised!'

Mom had never broken a promise before, so she turned around reluctantly and we went back home. I was relieved not

## THE FLIGHT HOME

to go to school and spent the whole day in the empty home sitting on the floor watching TV, which wasn't exactly my idea of fun but it was better than school. In the following days the temperature continued to go down but Mom didn't let us stay home anymore, and we stopped checking the thermometer.

Things at school remained the same. No matter how hard I tried, I couldn't find my place. By the time winter arrived, I was looking quite pale, particularly for someone with Mediterranean olive skin, and all my pants were feeling tight at the waist. One day Dad brought back some pictures of us he had printed at the Kodak shop on his way back from work. I was shocked to see how different I looked. My face was chubby, I had acne and I looked round everywhere, covered in thick layers of clothes. I looked again hoping it was just a bad angle and left the pictures on the table. I went upstairs to my parents' bathroom and decided to weigh myself. Being a skinny 50 kg. girl in Rio, I had never worried about my weight, but when I checked the scale, it showed 59 kg. I immediately stepped out biting my lower lip. It was a white analogue scale with a red arrow. I removed all my clothes and stepped back on the scale again contracting my tummy. This time it showed 58.5 kg.

I looked in the mirror at my naked body, pinching my underarms, my double chin and I started crying silently. I put my clothes back on, went back to my bedroom making sure no one saw me and I lay on my bed. When Mom called me for dinner, I said I had a headache and just wanted to sleep. I opened my Rio album, flicked through my old pictures and silent tears started rolling down my cheek. That night I dreamed in Portuguese.

Every day I woke up with the intention of getting fit again but by the time I returned home from school, I only had the energy to sit on the floor and watch TV. I even started to understand some Dutch after reading hours of subtitles.

I stopped weighing myself. It was useless. My skin also broke out with bad acne, partly due to the harsh weather, and partly due to the hormones of puberty and teen depression. I couldn't recognize the stranger in the mirror every morning. I didn't like what I saw so I avoided the mirrors, particularly full-body ones. I was like a beautiful pink balloon that deflated until it was reduced to its minimum expression, lying flat on the floor.

School breaks were dreadful. Everyone was rushing to their group of friends to sit together and eat their snacks or lunch, but I didn't have anyone to rush to, so I always took my time, procrastinating in front of my locker pretending to be busy unpacking my stuff. I didn't want to be seen spending the breaks alone, so I started to eat my lunch hiding in the bathroom, and no one missed me.

During school hours, I focused on learning and participating in class as this gave me purpose. I had the best scores in the subjects in French, but I was struggling with the subjects delivered in English like history, geography, and biology. Biology was the worst. Because it was so technical, I had to first translate the text into French in my head, then learn the new technical words, study the actual meaning, and then memorize the word in English. It was a long and painful process that drained my brain but at least it kept me busy.

In January 1996, I went into my first biology exam with Miss Robertson, a British teacher. It was the first time in my entire life I went into an exam feeling unprepared, although I had studied as much as I could. When the exam started, I tried to concentrate, and while my peers were focusing on their answers, I was trying to understand the questions. I was looking at the clock that was ticking furiously fast, and when the time was up, I hadn't had time to finish the exam. I waited until the other students left the classroom, and approached Miss Robertson's desk. She

## THE FLIGHT HOME

looked up at me and then back down at her papers, ignoring my presence. I hesitated and finally stuttered in my broken English, 'I didn't have time to finish because my English is not very good but I know the answers. Can I please have ten minutes extra to write them down?'

Raising an eyebrow, she looked at me and replied with a sarcastic tone, 'Well, this is a biology class, not an English class, right? I have to be fair to everyone.'

I felt my cheeks burn, muttered a thank you, and handed in my paper. I wanted to explain to her that I was trying my best and tell her the answers to the questions but the words didn't come out.

Without looking at me, she added with a firm tone, 'Please close the door on your way out.'

A week later she handed back the exams with some comments, mostly compliments to the other students. When it was my turn, she handed me the paper and said, 'Almost there.' I looked at it and there was a 4.5 written in red ink. Close to the 5 mark but not close enough to make it. Quickly I hid the exam under my thick biology book making sure I covered the red score from the other students.

A few weeks later, my biggest high school nightmare happened. Someone wrote a handwritten love letter on a piece of paper pretending it was me, with my name in the signature and a bunch of heart shapes. The letter was written in English and was full of intentional and silly grammar mistakes. The handwriting was hideous and Madame Combescure would have said it was written by a cat, but apparently, I was the author. It was addressed to a British boy called Richard who was also in biology class. Dounia told me about the letter and when I finally got hold of it, I was mortified. It looked childish and now everyone was thinking that the new girl had a crush on that boy

I barely knew.

The next day, Richard came to talk to me, and before he could say anything, I scolded him in my broken English, 'I didn't write that stupid letter. It's your silly friends.'

He started blushing and I saw his friends laughing at the scene from the corner of the break room. When the bell rang, it was time for biology class and I was now haunted not only by Miss Robertson and her biology molecules but also by Richard and the love letter. That day I learned the word prank.

After a few cold months of winter and a few more breaks in the bathroom, spring started to warm our cold spirits. Once a month Dad brought back letters from our friends in Brazil in the same brown leather suitcase he had in Rio. I kept on receiving ten-pages-long, handwritten letters from Sabrina, Marion, and Rachel, telling me about the cool parties, the concerts on the beach, the boys and all the fun. It was a bittersweet reminder of the life I was not living.

When summer arrived, I begged my parents to let me go to Rio on holiday, but Dad categorically forbade it, as he feared that if I went back aged of sixteen, I would never come back. Deep down, I think he was right ...

The summer holidays of 1996 were in Tenerife with my family, and the sun from the Atlantic gave me a boost of energy and a nice tan before going back to Alkmaar. After one year in Holland, my English was fluent and on day one of school, I wasn't the new girl anymore. I decided to sign up for aerobics classes at a local gym in Alkmaar and started going every day after school. I enjoyed the sweat, the dopamine, and the feeling of burning the toxins at the end of the workout. I still refused to jump on the scales, but slowly my jeans started to feel less tight and I felt lighter.

One day, I was packing my notebook from French class when

# THE FLIGHT HOME

I overheard Romain, a French boy from my class whisper to Matt who was sitting right behind me.

'She looks so different ... I think I might have a crush on her.'

I pretended not to hear it and went on packing my stuff. That afternoon I took my bike after school and went to the city center. I saw a beautiful flower dress in the window of one of my favorite shops, Escada, and I decided to try it on.

The salesgirl looked at me with a big smile and said, 'It looks stunning on you. You are so lucky to have golden skin.' I smiled and bought the dress.

I was now in the last year of high school and we were the cool kids, the ones getting ready to go to college. I still missed my friends and Rio, but I knew I only had one year to go before I would start university, so it was a countdown to get out of there. I came back from summer determined not to spend a single break in the toilet, not to feel pity for myself, and not to hide in the shadows.

I started to speak up more, reaching out to people during the break and that's how I became friends with Dounia. At first, we didn't have anything in common; she was the daughter of Moroccan immigrants, had lived in the Netherlands her whole life, and came from a very strict Muslim family. But the more time we spent together in class, and outside during the breaks, the more I liked her.

One day she told me, 'I thought you were really boring. It turns out you just had to warm up. You are hilarious and wicked smart.'

I started laughing and replied, 'You are not too bad either.'

Dounia was full of life, witty, and street-smart. She had long curly hair and big cheeky brown eyes. She was extroverted and loud, and her laugh was contagious. I had never met any Muslim girls before and she was the opposite of what I expected. She would often get in trouble in class for chatting and gossiping while Mr. Auclair was looking away but would do just fine on the exams. Plus, she spoke a bunch of languages: French, English, Dutch, Arabic, and German. So at least we had the language connection in common, as well as both of us having strict dads.

We started to hang out outside of school and became close friends. I always knew Dounia would do well in life because she had a positive, can-do attitude. I met her twenty years later in Dubai where she was living and working as a marketing director, and a few years after that in Hong Kong, when she came to visit while I was living on the Island. She hadn't changed a bit and had the same contagious energy.

I also made a few other friends. There were the two Italian Sergios, both born to Italian immigrants but raised in Alkmaar; Suzanne who was half Belgian and half Surinamese; Daphne who was Guatemalan-Dutch; and the English twins. One day, I was sitting with a few friends outside on the grass during the lunch break and I was speaking Italian with Sergio, French with Dounia, and English with the group. My classmate Amanda was staring at me for a while.

She asked, 'Veronica, how many languages do you speak?' I blushed as the entire conversation stopped and all the eyes were on me. I muttered, 'Five.' She looked surprised and added, 'That's amazing! You are the first polyglot I have ever met.'

I also started to hang out with a boy called Marlon, who was half Dutch, half Indian, and looked like a movie star. He was handsome and popular and played in the school band with the other cool guys. He was artistic and creative and everybody liked him. He had lost his dad when he was little, and he lived with his mom, Bonnie who was a lovely and charming Dutch lady. Marlon and I had nothing in common, but we clicked, and we loved to chat after school. I liked him but was too shy to tell him.

## THE FLIGHT HOME

I wasn't surprised when years later he told me he had moved to Los Angeles and was going through castings to become an actor. He had Hollywood written all over him.

When spring arrived in June 1996, the sun started to shine on my life. From May onwards, the days were much longer, there was light and sunshine until the evenings. People looked happier and smiled more and everyone was out-and-about on the streets, in the parks, and riding their bikes. Life was everywhere and it felt like a different world.

Alkmaar and Bergen were both very safe places and my parents encouraged me to join the other teenagers at night at the local club, called Palermo, where all the cool people from school went. My English was fluent and I had finally joined the cool crew and was invited to all the parties. I would hang out and dance with them and drink some alcohol we had sneaked from home in water bottles without Dad realizing it.

The best parties were the ones on the sand dunes, in Bergen, where we would light a fire, dance, drink, and chat until dawn. One Saturday evening, I was getting ready to go to a party and ride my bike there and back.

Mom looked at me when I went to the living room and said, 'You look great in that dress. You are glowing. It's great to see you be you again.'

I did a little model pose around with my hand on my hips and said, 'Alkmaar will never be Rio but it's not too bad. Plus you and Dad finally let me go out.'

Mom adjusted the strap on my dress and said, 'Have fun and make sure you ride back home with someone.'

'Yes, Mom! You sound like a broken record. Bye!' and I waved as I closed the door and headed toward my bike.

Weekends became more fun as Jose-Miguel, a Spanish guy from school sometimes invited a group of us for a sleepover at his place in Amsterdam, and we were allowed to go out into the Red-light district with all the sex shops and the famous sex windows street, check out the coffee shops, trying the occasional joint, and dance at the night clubs. I was only sixteen and I was finally starting to see the Amsterdam I had dreamed of when I left Rio.

In June 1997, I sat my baccalaureate exams. It was hours and hours of back-to-back exams in four different languages and I was exhausted by the end of each day. I had put in the hard work during the year, and it paid off. On graduation day, all students were invited to the ceremony in the main lobby of the school. They decorated the hall with white flowers and flags from all the European countries. It was the biggest day of the year and there were around 200 chairs for the guests, mostly parents, siblings, and teachers.

The school band, led by Marlon, opened the ceremony with a brilliant performance of piano and drums, followed by some readings and speeches. It was the most important day of my life as a student, with everyone dressed to impress with stunning gowns and elegant suits. Wearing a knee-length white dress, I was sitting in the front row, with all the other graduates. I looked behind me and saw Mom, Dad and Vicky. Dad gave me a thumbs-up and winked. I was nervously shaking my golden high heels as the adrenaline kicked in.

When the band finished playing, Marlon passed in front of me and whispered, 'That dress looks stunning on you.' I smiled and later that night checked the word "stunning" in the dictionary.

The Principal greeted everyone on stage in eight different languages and made a welcoming speech. He announced he was going to invite the top three students on stage to present each of them with a distinction award and then proceed to the entire class graduation, calling the students, one by one, to shake hands

# THE FLIGHT HOME

and pose for an official picture.

Although the exam results had been disclosed, no one knew the overall ranking, so all the students were anticipating the awards. Essi, my Finnish friend won the first award, and Razi, a Dutch boy whose parents were Pakistani, won the second award. When the Principal announced the third award, I heard, "Veronica Llorca Mendoza" on the speaker.

At first, I didn't react but seconds later, my heart started to beep fast like a ticking bomb. I turned around and saw that Vicky was rubbing her eyes, holding Mom's arm. She started laughing and made a frantic gesture with her hands, pointing toward the stage.

'Go, go!'

I walked toward the stage focusing on the stairs. When I reached the Principal, he shook my hand and said congratulations. I looked at the audience and smiled. I was standing tall, my classmates were clapping. I wasn't hiding in the bathroom. I wasn't hiding from the scales. I wasn't hiding any more.

# Chapter Five
## *The Last Chess Game – Courage*

My new life had a stamp on it: the city of Salamanca, Spain, and the date, October 1st, 1997. A couple of months earlier, I was discussing options for my university studies during dinner with Mom and Dad in Alkmaar.

'You will love Salamanca,' Dad said, 'it's the best university in Spain for law and the city is famous for its student life.'

I paused for a moment and replied calmly, 'I honestly don't feel like going to Spain. I don't feel Spanish. I speak like a foreigner and I have never studied Spanish. I'm going to be like a fish out of the water, again.'

After dinner, Mom came to my room and sat next to me on the bed. She convinced me to give Salamanca a try. I would be living in a dorm with other students and it would be an amazing experience.

'You are still seventeen, just give it a go, she said.' 'You can always choose to go somewhere else next year if you don't like it.'

Sighing in frustration I replied, 'I'm just tired of starting anew and being different. Sometimes I wish I had had a normal life, like everybody else. The other students will know I'm different from miles away and they will mock my accent.'

## THE FLIGHT HOME

Mom gently pushed my long dark hair behind my ear and said, 'One day you will look back and realize how lucky you were.'

When I first arrived in Salamanca, I was blown away by how beautiful the city was, with its two cathedrals, old and new, its majestic statues and elegant buildings made with a charming rose-pink old stone, the emblematic color of the city. The imposing Plaza Mayor, in the middle of the city, had hundreds of students walking around in different directions, speaking all sorts of languages.

The old town is mostly for pedestrians, particularly at night when it becomes a flow of energetic young people, hungry to conquer the world. And I was one of them. I enrolled in a law degree because my parents convinced me that it would open many doors in the future. I wasn't particularly interested in law but I was happy to become independent and live away from home.

On the first day at the dorm, management invited all the students to the main lobby. The director Pedro asked each of the forty students to stand, make a short introduction and share their city of origin. As the students began to introduce themselves, I observed curiously, they were all Spanish and came from all over the country, mostly from small towns I had never heard of before. There wasn't a single foreigner. When it was my turn, Pedro said, 'And now we have the girl who speaks five languages. Veronica, please introduce yourself and tell us where you come from.' The room became silent, and I felt the students screening me from head to toe. My cheeks were blushing but I acted cool and smiled. I said what I had been nervously rehearsing in my mind, 'Hi, I'm Veronica and I am from the Canary Islands but I grew up in France and Brazil and just moved from the Netherlands.'

Some people started clapping, others were just staring at me, and the student whose turn was right after mine said with a cheeky grin, 'Great, I get to go after the smart chick. My name is Fernando, I'm from Malaga and I only speak Spanish.'

'Poorly!' yelled someone from the background, and we all started laughing.

After the meeting, a blond girl approached me and said, 'Your story is so cool, Rio sounds amazing.'

Her name was Silvia and her room was just next to mine. She was also in her first year of law school and we became inseparable. This time around, I made friends quickly. The other students were fascinated by my story and the languages I spoke, as most of them had only visited nearby countries in Europe.

During the week, we were busy attending class in the morning, and studying in the library in the afternoon and, by the weekend, it was all about partying. Salamanca was the opposite of Alkmaar. The city was busy day and night with hundreds of clubs and pubs, all offering deals to students.

Life in the dorm was the best part of university because I was living with my best friends, no parents, and no curfew. I could come in at whatever time I wanted, or not come back at all, and no one would raise an eyebrow. Every week was packed with excitement, new bars, alcohol, and dancing. Plus the perks like *Happy Wednesday*, where girls were offered drinks for free in most bars. It was heaven on earth, with a bunch of law books.

Every month my parents sent me an allowance for my personal expenses but I found an interesting way of making some extra cash. One of the very first things I did when I started university was to enroll myself at a local gym called Pasadena, 500 meters from the dorm. I joined the aerobics classes on a daily basis, usually at 6:00 p.m. after I had finished studying for the day. Some days I would do two back-to-back classes.

One day, we were waiting for Karen, the aerobics instructor,

## THE FLIGHT HOME

and after ten minutes, the gym owner, Tony, came to apologize and explained that Karen had had an emergency and would not be able to deliver the class. We all looked at each other with disappointment, and some girls started to pack up to go.

Without thinking about it too much, I turned to Tony, and in front of everyone I asked, 'I'm not an instructor but would you mind if I took the class today? I have done aerobics for a few years. It might not be a perfect class but I can get a good sweat out of us, rather than sending everyone home upset.'

Tony was a bit puzzled by the proposal, but he also looked amused. He looked around and addressed the group, 'Ladies, raise your hands if you want to stay.' To my surprise, all eight girls raised their hands. Tony shrugged his shoulders and, pointing toward the mirror said, 'The floor is yours. Keep everyone safe!'

I walked toward the front of the room without any preparation or choreography in mind. I picked the first CD I found on the side shelf, *Top Hits from the 90s*. The music started playing and I looked at the group with a smile while pulling my long hair back into a ponytail. *You got this*, I told myself. I kneeled to tie up my shoelaces while improvising the choreography in my head and stood back up, looked straight in the mirror, and yelled with a firm, military voice, 'Follow me in 3, 2, 1!'

Fifty minutes later, I finished the class and the girls started clapping. Everyone was sweating, some girls approached me and high-fived me, or thanked me.

'That was awesome,' I heard someone say in the background. I packed my black Nike gym bag and as I was ready to leave the gym, Tony stopped me at reception.

'Amazing job today! People loved it. It seems you gave them a good sweat and there were no accidents. I have a couple of openings in the afternoon. Would you be interested in joining as an aerobics instructor? 1,500 pesetas a lesson, Monday,

Wednesday, and Friday.'

Without hesitation, I said, 'Yes,' remembering my days in Alkmaar.

That night I called home. Mom, Vicky, and Dad were still living in Alkmaar and international calls were expensive. Once a week, I went to a students café where I purchased a phone card which gave me credit for a fifteen-minute call. I told Mom the story of becoming an improvised aerobics teacher.

'I told you,' she laughed, 'what doesn't kill you makes you stronger. You would never have put your hand up if it wasn't for Holland!'

Mom was always right.

I was having the time of my life in Salamanca. I had made a big group of friends, earned top grades at university, and had enough money to party throughout the whole month. When summer arrived in 1998, my family moved back to the Canary Islands, this time to an island called Fuerteventura, near the Moroccan coast. The island had a big port which received cargo from Spain and overseas and Dad had been appointed as the Chief of Customs. I landed at the airport of Fuerteventura in July, curious to discover our new home.

Dad gave me a hug and teased me, 'I hope your grades are as good as mine were.'

I pulled out my grades report, handed it to him, and said with a teasing smile, 'Better, Dad, check this out.'

He took a quick glance at the report and added, 'Congratulations. The apple doesn't fall far from the tree.' I laughed. I didn't care about the grades as much as I cared about making Dad proud. I looked through the window as we were driving to my parents' new home in the small town of Puerto del Rosario and immediately fell in love with the island. The air was dry, the sky was deep blue and we were surrounded by white

## THE FLIGHT HOME

sand dunes and crystalline waters.

With my hand making waves out of the window, I said out loud, 'From Alkmaar to paradise. Seems like a good trade-off to me!'

Summer went by and in October I started my second year of law. I loved my new life. Salamanca kept me busy with studying and partying and Fuerteventura was my little family oasis to relax and go on holiday. I was excited to move to a flat with Silvia and a medical student called Rosa. When I showed them the pictures from Fuerteventura, they both marveled.

'Wow, you really seem to have it all: the brains, looks, languages, and a perfect family on an island. You are just missing a boyfriend!'

We laughed and opened a bottle of white wine to celebrate the beginning of the school year.

Sometime in my fourth year, I heard about Erasmus. It was a public scholarship that granted European students a monthly allowance to study abroad for one year, at another European university. To qualify, students were required to have top grades and speak the language of the country. I decided to apply and picked Italy as the destination.

Once the results of the language test came out, the program coordinator congratulated me, 'Well done. You got the top score in Italian so you can choose any university in Italy.'

My head started spinning. I was about to move countries by myself again, and I had to make a decision. I skimmed through the list of cities — Rome, Pisa, Milan, Florence — and finally ticked the box next to the city of Bologna. I was ready to venture into the unknown.

I landed in Bologna in September 2001, and took a taxi to Via Dante, next to the *Giardini Margherita* (Margherita Gardens). It dropped me at the gate of my new life. I looked up, and it was an old walk-up building with six floors where everything was old with thick wooden doors, high ceilings, and massive dark glass windows. There was something nostalgic and authentic about it, and I immediately loved my new Italian home. I carried my heavy brown leather suitcase up the stairs and knocked at the door.

The owner, Sergio, was a young Italian lawyer who had converted the four-bedroom flat into a university apartment where he only hosted girls, mostly Erasmus students. I was convinced he earned more as a landlord than as a lawyer because the rent was not cheap. Everything was expensive in Bologna, so I decided to share my room with a stranger, as I wasn't planning to stay at home very much anyway.

Linda was friendly and fun and I was the lucky one who had an Italian native as a roommate, so my Italian would improve really fast. She was a beautiful, bubbly, blue-eyed brunette from a small town called Pistoia and she was also in Bologna for her studies. The remaining rooms were occupied by four girls: a German, French, Belgian, and another Spanish girl. It would have made a great movie with six female students under one roof because every day there was new gossip and drama.

There was also a small room in the flat that didn't even qualify to be a bedroom, as it fitted a mattress, which if laid on, and arms were stretched from side to side, would touch both walls. It became a room for siblings, one-night stands, and drunk friends who passed out. Every other night we had a new guest and it was first in, first served. Waking up in the morning and bumping into a stranger in the corridor became the norm, especially on the weekends, and no one ever complained, as we were Erasmus.

My favorite part of the flat was the kitchen. There was no living room as I suppose it had been reconverted into a bedroom to maximize the earnings for the owner. Therefore the kitchen

## THE FLIGHT HOME

was used for everything—the living room, dining area, gossip room, and the actual kitchen. It was the meeting point for whoever was up for a chat in the morning or late at night after partying at the bars. There was no TV but we had a DVD player that mostly played Italian songs. The famous Italian singer *Paolo Conte* was a favorite, especially in the mornings and that's how I learned most of his lyrics. The kitchen had a glass and wooden door that led onto a tiny little balcony that could fit two people maximum at a time. Because we were on the sixth floor floor and Bologna didn't have any tall buildings, it gave us a fantastic panoramic view of the city, with all its little red roofs.

Besides perfecting my Italian language skills, I also learned their expressive hand language. Italians have the extraordinary ability to describe anything with their two hands, without having to say a word. To sound like a native, we had to nail the "Mamma Mia" hand expression, which can be used interchangeably in situations such as surprise, disappointment, happiness, astonishment, and anger. It works 99 percent of the time, particularly if it is said dramatically while moving and shaking both hands with all fingers coming together and facing the skies.

The best part of being a girl in Italy was ... being a girl in Italy. No matter whether a woman was tall, short, blond, brunette, skinny, or curvy, they automatically were called *Bella*, by men. Italian men love to be charming and flirtatious, and whenever I went out on a date, each man would be the most courteous and flattering in the world. From opening the door to paying for absolutely everything, even if I insisted on doing it the Dutch way, as I had been taught in the Netherlands. I felt like the ultimate Cinderella in a 21st Century fairy tale. Of course, a couple of days later I would bump into the same charming prince who would be putting together the same show with another *Bella* girl.

That was the game, and I played by the rules by embracing the *Bella*, and the compliments, all the while knowing that the prince in this fairy tale was not going to find me after midnight because he was going to a different ball to look for a new Cinderella.

I couldn't have chosen a better way to end my university life. I learned a lot about Italian law but more importantly, I learned about its culture and its history. I visited stunning towns from Sienna to Padova, Verona, Rimini, Florence, Milan, and Rome. Trains were not expensive and very often, we would sneak in without a ticket and jump off at any random station as soon as a ticket controller stepped on the train. I made Italian friends and discovered twenty different types of pasta and pizza, and that putting pineapple in your pizza is a crime under Italian law. On Sundays in summer, I always skipped lunch and replaced it with an artisanal two-scoops gelato, a total calorie bomb full of goodness.

In June 2002, I traveled back to Salamanca to attend the graduation ceremony with my law classmates. I was excited to see them all after my year abroad and receive our degrees together after five years of studies. Silvia and I were sitting together, waiting for our names to be called on stage.

As the awards ceremony was about to start, she whispered in my ear, 'I don't know how you do it. You just make moving countries and learning languages look so easy. I wish I was that brave.'

The dean called our names and the students in our row stood up to go on the stage. He welcomed everyone and added, 'Congratulations, you are all law graduates now. Some of you will become lawyers, others judges or attorneys. You might end up doing something completely different, but one thing is for sure: your degree will help you open new doors.'

After the ceremony, I flew to Fuerteventura without knowing

## THE FLIGHT HOME

what doors to knock on. I didn't want to stay in Spain and start climbing the corporate ladder as an intern, or work for free at some prestigious consulting company, as many of my friends dreamed of. I wanted to find something that would give me wings to travel the world so I enrolled into a master's degree in international business in Madrid. The tuition was very expensive and I was granted a scholarship for 50 percent of the amount, thanks to my academic results. The university would grant me the remaining 50 percent if I ranked top three at the end of the year. Dad's best friend Jose generously offered me to stay in a small studio he owned in the center of Madrid, so my adventure in the Spanish capital began. I was ready to give it all, just like during my university years — study hard, play hard, and continue with the carefree student lifestyle by now I had totally mastered.

I had been to Madrid dozens of times throughout the years, but always as a tourist, or on my way to the Canary Islands. Now the big capital was my new home, and I was thrilled to discover every little corner and start a new life again.

On the first day, I took the subway to attend my master's class. I was intrigued to meet my new colleagues, make new friends, learn all about international business, and find a way to move overseas with a high-income job. My friends in Salamanca told me I was dreaming.

'You will have to suck it up, just like the rest of us, and climb the bloody ladder,' my classmate Victor had told me on graduation day.

I didn't say anything. I just smiled knowing that I would find a way to continue my journey around the world.

I entered the classroom and looked around. It was easy to see I was the youngest. When the introductions began, I found that most students were in their early thirties and came from various countries in Central and South America. Many had inherited a family business and as the new generation, wanted to modernize, and expand it overseas. I also met a very fun guy from Greece called Manolis, and a Chinese student called Roy. He was the first Chinese person I had ever met, besides the Chinese waiters in restaurants. He spoke very little Spanish and I had no idea what he was doing there, but he was always smiling.

On Thursday of the first week, I was on my way to class when my silver Nokia phone rang. It was Mom, and I picked it up while packing my handbag to leave home.

'Hi Mom, can I call you later? I'm on my way to class.'

There was silence on the line and Mom said, 'Hi. I need to talk to you.'

Her voice sounded deep and broken. I didn't recognize that tone. It didn't sound like Mom. I had a flashback and mentally traveled to Rio when I had seen her cry for the first time.

She continued, 'Your dad is sick. We just took a flight to Madrid this morning and he was admitted to the hospital.'

The words were hammering my brain, I stuttered, 'Sick, hospital ... what do you mean Mom, how sick?'

'He's in intensive care at the hospital. He's in good hands and his condition is stable. Please come as soon as you can and I will tell you more. I'm sending you a text with the address. Love you.'

I mumbled a few words and hung up the phone. I sat on the beige leather couch in the living room, trying to make sense of the scattered pieces of information. I remained silent, listening to the sound of my heart beating faster, I could barely swallow. I stood up but felt dizzy and leaned my hand against the wall to regain my balance. I took a deep breath and went to the bathroom, and splashed cold water on my face.

I looked in the mirror and told myself, 'You can do this. He will be fine. It's Dad.'

## THE FLIGHT HOME

I jumped on the subway as I had done the previous three days to go to my classes, but this time I was taking a different route, just as my life was about to also. I looked around wondering if the strangers could see the fear in my eyes. When I arrived at the hospital, I took the lift to the third-floor intensive care unit. It was cold and sterile and everything was stark white.

The lift seemed to go on forever, and as the door opened, I saw Mom. She was pale and skinny, like someone who hadn't slept or eaten for days.

I hugged her and she said, 'Dad is really sick, he was just diagnosed with cancer but the doctors said he's in good hands.'

She continued talking about the cancer and the treatment he was going through but I only heard scattered words like saturnism, tubes, and morphine, as it was all a blur. I couldn't understand my own language. I was just processing sounds, images, thoughts, and feelings. It was like waking up from a dream and not remembering anything. A nurse passing by stared at Mom and me, and we made eye contact. She smiled the way nurses smile when they see a relative of a terminally ill patient. Vicky came out of the bathroom, gave me a hug, and started crying on my shoulder. When I looked at her, she shook her head without saying a word. Silence.

As I walked along the long corridor, some of the doors were open and I saw very old and fragile people confined to their beds. I stopped in front of room number 305, paralyzed for a moment. I knocked softly but there was no response. I opened the door gently and there was Dad, lying on the bed. When he saw me, his big eyes sparkled with light. Although he was only fifty-nine, he looked like he had aged twenty years overnight, and looked like an eighty-year-old man. He was weak, all the little veins in his eyes were bright red.

I wanted to hide my shock but my body was paralyzed. I kept

on screening him, as I bit my lips. He had lost around 15 kg. or more and I could see the shape of his bones under his very thin, pale skin. He tried to mutter something with a smile, but he could barely speak and I couldn't understand what he said. He had tubes everywhere. I looked at him for five seconds and did my best to mimic a smile.

'Hi, Dad.'

I was going to say something else but instead, I turned around and left the room, letting the door slap itself behind me. I wanted to run far away, as far as I could. I wanted to run to the mountains in the Pyrenees and hug my dad in his office. I wanted to show him my school report in French, even if he didn't understand it. I wanted to play a chess league with him, I wanted to run to Rio and hug him in his Hawaiian shirt. I wanted to smell his cologne one more time but all I could smell was the hideous, bitter hospital scent of antiseptic, and cleaning products. I wanted to scream as loud as I could. Instead, I found a corner at the end of the long corridor and cried, and cried, until my tears had dried and I had no more strength to keep crying.

I knew it was the end of his life. No matter what the doctors had promised or planned, I could feel it. I didn't have to talk to the nurses about his illness, because my whole heart knew what was happening the moment I saw Dad's eyes, and he knew it too. I closed my eyes one last time to picture that little girl on Dad's lap. I opened my eyes and I saw a big white clock on the wall and wanted to stop it and send it back in time but it kept ticking, one second after the next.

I closed my fists and told myself, 'Come on, go back inside. You can do it, you have to do it. Be brave.' And so I did.

I opened the door a second time, took a deep breath, and sat calmly next to Dad. He whispered a few words in spite of all the tubes, and I sensed he could understand everything that was going on. So I told him stories from our life together to distract him, and make him smile.

I told him about Madrid, I reminded him of silly stories of Rio, and I found the strength to smile while I was holding his weak hand. I told him about my master's studies.

'Dad, I'm the youngest one there, but I promise you I will get the highest score. You have to get out of here to be my date on graduation day when they give me the award.' I talked for an hour, hoping that perhaps if I didn't stop talking, he would stay there with me, listening.

The following two days were a blur of different shades of grey. The minutes seemed to last hours, and although Dad was still here with us, I could barely recognize him. Mom was beside him day and night, spending most nights as she drifted in and out of sleep beside him on a sofa. I was not able to think about the future, as I was too afraid to look beyond today, and the clock on the wall was ticking fast.

On October 17th, 2002, Dad was gone; the last little flame had burnt out. I spent that night awake, crying, and trying to avoid falling asleep because I wanted to relive in my mind all the happy times together around the world as a happy little family. I wanted to recreate every little moment with as much detail as possible, remembering the exact words we spoke, what I was wearing, and the smells surrounding me. The more I could reconstruct every little piece of our past, the more present Dad was in me.

The funeral took place on Saturday morning and there I was, saying goodbye to Dad at the age of twenty-two. Dad always said that he wanted to be cremated, so we followed his wish. Inside the small church, Vicky could not stop crying throughout the entire ceremony. I cried many tears too, but only inside, silently. We were left with a broken heart and Dad's ashes, as a reminder that he was still with us but in a different way.

Ironically Mom's forty-third birthday was the next day. Vicky, Mom, and I were staying in my little studio, and we had barely slept.

Vicky looked at me and said, 'You look like a zombie.'

I gave her a hug and said, 'That makes two of us,' and we laughed between our tears.

I looked at Mom and said, 'Mom, I know the last thing you want is to celebrate but it's your birthday and Dad would love for you to have a nice day. Let's go to the pizzeria around the corner. We owe him that.'

We got dressed, walked out of the door, and ate pizza. His best friend Jose and his wife Teresa joined us. We talked, laughed, and we cried too. We all shared stories about Dad, mostly fun stories.

'To Dad, to all the good memories and to everything you have done for us,' I said, and we all raised our glasses of champagne and cheered.

Up until then, I had always considered myself privileged for having the education I received, for having traveled the world, for having had the opportunity to learn languages, and to go to good schools. However the first time someone referred to me as an orphan, I realized that I was wrong — my biggest privilege had been having Mom and Dad by my side since I was a child. And that privilege was suddenly taken away from me without warning.

A few months after the funeral, Mom was back in Fuerteventura, living by herself in a small flat as she had been evicted from the customs house. One day, on a sunny afternoon, she hired a local fisherman to take her on his small fishing boat along the coast of the Atlantic Ocean. She waited until sunset, and when the sun was fading on the horizon, she scattered Dad's ashes into the sea, dedicating him a prayer.

# THE FLIGHT HOME

She had met him on an island, they had traveled the world with their two daughters, and she was now back to say goodbye one last time, closing the circle.

Eight months later, I went on stage for graduation day. The master's director called my name for the first award. I took it with a smile, I looked up and said, 'This one's for you, Dad.'

# CHAPTER SIX
## *The Orphan – Hope*

Two months after the funeral, Vicky, Mom, and I reunited in Fuerteventura to spend Christmas of 2002 together, our first as a family of three. I was always excited to see the first piece of land of the Canary Islands from my window seat. The flight from Madrid was almost three hours and I spent the entire time looking through the window, occasionally wiping a tear. The sky was deep blue as I remembered it, but this time I felt a void upon landing. Mom and Vicky collected me at the airport with a big smile. They had both lost weight but their tanned skin gave them a healthy look. We hugged as we always did but it was a different hug, one filled with mixed emotions. We didn't stop talking in the car about small things, in an attempt to fill the void with words. We were learning how to be a family again and today was chapter one.

We parked on the street of Mom's new place. It was a new development in a working-class neighborhood in the capital of the island, Puerto del Rosario with little charm or soul. I looked around but it was all bricks and buildings. There was a bar just next to it that smelled like tobacco and had a couple of vending machines inside and some men watching football on the TV screen. The building had no lift and we walked up the stairs to

## THE FLIGHT HOME

the third floor. Mom opened the wooden door and let us in. She asked joyfully, 'What do you think of my new place?'

I walked around with curiosity as I inspected the flat. The decoration was cozy and I could recognize some furniture and paintings from Rio but the flat was small and a bit dark. It missed the warmth and light of all our previous homes.

I replied teasing her, 'Mom, you should spoil yourself and rent a nice place close to the sea. You could walk along the beach in the morning.'

Mom suddenly looked uneasy. I felt guilty and immediately apologized, 'I'm sorry, I didn't mean it. I know you had to vacate the customs house in only a few days, pack everything, and find a new place. You have done amazingly well.'

My words didn't alleviate her serious expression. She was wearing blue jeans and a white cotton T-shirt that marked her prominent bones. She was as skinny as in Madrid.

She joined her hands together and said with a deep tone, 'I need to talk to you both.' Vicky and I looked at each other puzzled, trying to find some hints of what was going on. She sat on the Ikea grey couch and, instinctively, Vicky and I joined her.

'We are going to have to make some financial adjustments. Your dad made some bad investments in the past and he left some loans behind. There's not a lot of money left.'

The words hit me like an unexpected truck coming from the opposite direction. We had always been well-off and money had never been an issue. We had always gone to private schools, had two cars and went for dinner in nice places. I was trying to make sense of it all but there was no sense to be made. The pieces of the puzzle didn't fit. Vicky was sitting next to me on the couch. She looked confused and scared and grabbed my hand without saying a word.

'How bad is it, Mom?' I asked pragmatically, in a matter-of-fact tone.

Mom didn't reply at first. She attempted to smile, her hazel eyes became teary and all I could hear was the word "bankrupt" before she burst into tears. Vicky and I sat closer to her and comforted her while she was sobbing. I gently rubbed her back.

'It's OK Mom. It can't be that bad, we will get through it. I will finish my master's in a few months. I will get a job and will help repay the debt. It's just money.'

Mom talked for over an hour. It was that bad. It was worse. Dad had borrowed big amounts of money over the years through loans and the interest rates had started to creep up year after year. It was not one isolated loan from one bank. It was multiple loans from various banks all over Spain. After the banks had received the notification of Dad's passing, they started to call Mom daily and harass her over the phone to repay the capital and the interest, which had become larger than the capital itself. Mom had calculated it was over 500,000 Euros. The amount was astronomical.

Her mobile phone started ringing, the caller read "unknown". She didn't pick up and sighed. I composed myself, cleared my throat and asked, 'Are they going to call Vicky and me too?'

Fortunately, the debt didn't pass on to Vicky and me as long as we didn't accept any inheritance. And there was no inheritance. We didn't have any assets, property, or savings. Our only income was Mom's pension as a widow, but the state had ordered its partial seizure. She also had a small salary from working part time at the Duty-Free Shop at the airport as a casual worker. Overnight, my mother had gone from living the dream, owning a diplomatic red passport, spending holidays in nice resorts, and having drivers in armored cars, to being bankrupt. There was a somber silence. I remembered my friend Rosa saying that I had it all, and how ironic that felt now that I had nothing.

# THE FLIGHT HOME

After the initial shock, a sense of calmness took over. Mom had stopped crying and I could feel her relief. She had finally let go of the burden she had secretly carried for years.

I held Mom's hand and said, 'The only thing we can't change is the fact that Dad is gone. Everything else is just material stuff. Money comes and goes. Vicky and I are adults and we are just about to finish our studies and this place is not too bad. You will bring some glamour to the neighborhood. It can really use some.'

We started laughing and the sound of our laughter lifted the burden of being bankrupt. It was almost 2:00 p.m. and I went to the Chinese restaurant downstairs and ordered some takeaway for lunch. We always had the exact combination: spring rolls, sweet and sour pork, wantons, and fried rice. The bill arrived and it was 18 Euros. I checked the receipt and started reviewing the items. Suddenly, 18 Euros felt like a lot of money. Once back home, we enjoyed the food. Mom opened a bottle of white wine, we chatted, we teased each other and nothing reminded us that we were bankrupt. In my mind, it was just an ugly word.

New Year's Eve arrived and we said goodbye to 2002. Starting a new year forced me into a flashback of Dad across different countries. I pictured all the versions of Dad I had ever known, from my strong and muscular dad to the strict dad who was always scolding me as a teenager and the fragile dad confined to a hospital bed. They all gave way to a new dad who was just a mix of all of these in my heart. When the clock announced midnight, following the Spanish tradition, we all ate our twelve grapes, one for each month of the year and I made my wish: to get out of bankruptcy.

2003 was a lonely year in Madrid. Having just moved there, I didn't know anyone and my colleagues were mostly strangers. I didn't tell anyone I had lost my dad as I didn't need eyes of pity on me. I isolated myself in the world of books, allowing the other students to believe I didn't like to be social or go out. At some point, I realized I was no longer being invited to the parties. I overheard comments like, 'She is married to her books' and I felt excluded but deep down it was a relief as I didn't have to make up excuses anymore. It was just me and my date with grief.

Mom discovered there was a state-funded financial allowance for children of deceased civil servants and I said I would find out some more. I went into the official building one cold morning in January before my classes. It was an old majestic building in downtown Madrid with a wooden door and very high ceilings that amplified the echo of my high heels. The lady at the reception welcomed me and I enquired about the terms of the support.

'Who is the beneficiary?' she asked.

I hesitated. 'The beneficiary?' I muttered, slightly uncomfortable.

'Yes, who is the orphan?'

I stood silently in front of her, repeating the word orphan in my head.

The lady saw the look on my face and added, 'My condolences, I'm sorry for your loss. I will bring you a glass of water.'

She came back with a glass of water and a leaflet with all the information. I flicked through it looking at the pictures and reading the titles. Vicky and I were entitled to some financial help and reimbursement for school materials and clothes as long as we obtained top grades at school. I filled out the form, ticked the orphan box, and handed it back to her. It was just another ugly word, I thought to myself.

The months went by but Madrid never became home. I didn't make friends and I never knew what the nightlife was like. As the school year was coming to an end, I knew I desperately needed to find a job. The prospects in Spain were disheartening, with skyrocketing unemployment, an abundance of young graduates,

## THE FLIGHT HOME

and a lack of qualified jobs. I couldn't afford a local internship; I needed the money. That's when I heard about a government-sponsored program called ICEX for the first time. Although it was an internship, it was extremely competitive and well-paid because it was funded by the state. The interns were sent abroad for one year to work for the Spanish Trade Commission anywhere around the world.

It sounded like my dream job. I decided to apply for it and I studied hard for the exams on top of my regular studying for the master's. The competition was ferocious with over one thousand candidates from all over the country competing for 150 coveted spots. I passed one exam after the other and watched the list of candidates shrink as they were eliminated. When it was time to take the language exams, I applied for English, French, Italian, Portuguese, and German. I passed them all.

In June 2003, the final results were published online after one month of exams and I was over the moon to be in the top five and be the first female on the list. It was time to start laying the bricks of my future. The last phase of the process was a panel interview. I went in not knowing where I would be sent. All I knew was that I needed that opportunity and I was ready to fight for it. It was our ticket out of bankruptcy, out of Madrid, out of the smell of hospitals. It was my ticket to a brand-new life.

I was waiting in the corridor of the ICEX building with other candidates when the secretary called my name. I entered the room, and a group of five men and women sitting along a long wooden table welcomed me. They were chatting and the atmosphere was relaxed. I took a seat and after greeting me, the President of the Tribunal initiated the conversation.

'Congratulations on your results. We are very impressed, particularly with your languages.' I didn't hide my smile. He continued, 'We have decided to assign you one of the most interesting business destinations and also one of the best-paid ones.' My brain immediately started spinning. I was thinking it might be New York or London when he suddenly announced, 'Shanghai. It's the city of the future, and the Chinese economy is booming. Well done, it's the most exciting destination of the program. Before going to China, you will spend three months in Taiwan to learn Mandarin. Congratulations, Miss Llorca.'

I thanked them and left the room, closing the door behind me. China? I was puzzled, confused, and disappointed. I would have expected any other vibrant city, from Miami or Sydney to anywhere in Europe. I had never thought of China and the news on TV about China was always dark and full of controversy.

I left the building and called Mom. She had been waiting for my call impatiently and before I could say anything, she exclaimed, 'So, I bet they assigned you an exciting country!'

'No, Mom. It's China. The last place on Earth I want to go to. China,' I replied with anger and frustration.

Mom was shocked as well but she told me to take a deep breath and just analyze the situation. She convinced me to look at it as an opportunity. China was indeed the factory of the world, and one year there would be an experience in my CV and my life.

She added, 'You have always loved a challenge. Don't shy away from it. It might be the best thing that ever happens to your career. Plus I'm sure you will love learning Chinese and getting paid for it.'

Confused, I hung up the phone and headed straight into the first cyber-café I found. I Googled Shanghai and spent the next two hours browsing, learning about the city, and taking notes. I was fascinated by the pictures of the high-rises, the development of the country, and how the economy was booming at a double-digit pace. I didn't know anyone in China or anyone who had ever been to China. I thought of Roy, my Chinese colleague from

## THE FLIGHT HOME

the master's, and how brave he had been traveling to Spain to study without barely knowing the language.

The next day I woke up excited and full of energy. I went for a run around the Retiro Park and after I came home, I signed my acceptance letter and sealed my future with a China stamp. I was ready for the unknown.

# Chapter Seven
## A One-way Ticket to China – Curiosity

On the 1st of October 2003, I landed in Taipei on a one-way ticket. All my belongings were in my brown leather suitcase and an envelope with 600 Euros Mom had lent me. I would receive my first salary from the Spanish Government at the end of the month. The flight from Madrid was the longest I had ever taken, yet I had barely slept. I kept peeking through the window, and counting the hours left to land in Asia, the land of my future life.

A minivan was waiting for us at the airport to take us to our student dorm on the outskirts of Taipei. Among the fourteen interns, only three were girls –Nuria, Cecilia, and me. The moment we landed, we became friends.

As we started driving, I heard Yago, one of the male interns, yell from the back, 'What the hell, everything is in Chinese! Look at those red characters on the walls. It looks scary.'

The minivan window was open, and I could smell the tropics, the thick humidity, and the scent of urban rain. Taipei was a city full of life, noise, and chaos. It had a soul. Our driver, an old Chinese man with grey hair, explained that the public signs related to the SARS virus. Earlier in 2003, Taiwan had reported a series of outbreaks that had led to several casualties, and warnings were still displayed on the street.

## THE FLIGHT HOME

I immediately fell in love with the Chinese language. The elegant strokes were fascinating and alienating, as I had never been to a country where I couldn't read anything before. There were no English signs, and I realized how helpless I was. I couldn't read, say or understand anything. I was illiterate in a new country I knew little about, yet that feeling gave me energy and motivation. I had something big to accomplish. My friends in Spain had insisted that learning Chinese was impossible. I just nodded back in agreement, knowing I would prove them wrong.

We settled into the dorm, and I was assigned a room with Nuria, who came from a village near Barcelona. It was Saturday morning, so we had a weekend before we started Chinese classes on Monday morning. We took a quick shower to wash off the jetlag, and a few of us headed toward the subway to explore downtown Taipei.

As we exited Taipei station, I was blown away by a spectacle of neon lights, electronic music, and people.

'Wow,' I said in awe, 'I didn't expect Taipei to be so modern. It's like we have been transported into the future.'

Everything was bright, colorful, and vibrant. The streets were full of trendy young people who looked like models from Asian magazines. Guys, in particular, had funky hairstyles, and many wore blue or green eye lenses. Girls looked like Asian versions of Barbie dolls with long fake eyelashes, hair extensions, and extravagant makeup.

'This is like a movie,' Nuria said while we marveled at the spectacle of lights and sounds. We wandered around randomly, purchased water and snacks at a 7/11 convenience store, and returned to the dorm after eating a cup of noodles in a small shop. We turned on the TV, but everything was in Chinese. I wondered how long it would take me to understand what they were saying.

On Monday morning, the school minivan took us to the Taipei Language Institute, and we met our teachers who were waiting in the lobby. The head teacher, Miss Gu, was a tall and elegant Taiwanese woman dressed in black. Her green bracelets caught my attention. She welcomed everyone in English with a warm smile.

'Welcome to Taipei. You will be immersed in the Chinese language and culture during the next three months. Make the most of this opportunity as China is the country of the future, and speaking Chinese will be a huge advantage for you.'

We then started our first class, and I listened attentively as Miss Gu asked us to repeat some sounds after her.

'La, la, la, and la,' she vocalized, moving her hands up and down like an orchestra director with explaining that Mandarin has four different tones.

Cecilia laughed as she mimicked the sounds and said, 'They sound exactly the same. It's like singing opera.'

Miss Gu replied kindly, 'With some practice, you will start to notice the difference. Each "la" means something else, depending on the tone. "La" means spicy, and "la" means pulling. Can you tell the difference?'

I nodded discreetly, although they sounded just the same to me. The guys laughed in the background, pretending to be opera singers, while I quietly rehearsed the different tones of "la". After school, I found a local coffee shop nearby and decided to study the Chinese words from my first lesson and repeat the new sounds. When I checked my watch, two hours had passed, and I rushed back to the dorm.

Later in the week, I joined Javier and Cecilia to open a bank account downtown so we could have our salary transferred at the end of the month. We went to the local branch of a Taiwanese bank, and while waiting in the lobby, we noticed

## THE FLIGHT HOME

that the corporate mascot of the bank was a big blue cartoon, similar to the Japanese cartoon, Doraemon. The blue mascot was everywhere, in their advertisements, at the entrance, and there was even a giant one at the door welcoming customers, just like Mickey Mouse greeting customers at Disneyland.

Javier bluntly pointed at it. 'Should we trust Doraemon with our money?' he asked sarcastically. Shrugging our shoulders, Cecilia and I giggled. Later, I learned that many Asian countries have a big cartoon culture, similar to Japanese Manga. Diana, one of the Taiwanese assistants at the Spanish Trade Commission in Taipei, had a collection of Hello Kitty dolls she proudly displayed on her desk, even though she was in her thirties. There was even a Hello Kitty café, which was always busy with adults dressed in red and pink Hello Kitty outfits and accessories. Later that afternoon, we went to a cyber café sent Mom my first email from Asia.

'Hi, Mom. I made it! Taipei is so exciting. Every day I learn something new, and I love the experience. I sometimes feel like a fish out of water but I'm so lucky to have this opportunity. It's just like a movie.'

'I'm learning to eat with chopsticks, although the food here is so different from the Chinese food in Spain. I have started drinking hot water, too, just like the locals, and learning about all the different teas. The other interns are really nice and fun, and we have already bonded. I guess we have no option as we are the only foreigners here.'

'I'm so lucky to be here, and I love my Chinese classes. It's hard, but I'm studying a lot, and I will be able to speak it fluently within a year. I haven't seen the nightlife yet, but here is a picture of us in front of Taipei 101, the tallest building in Taiwan.'

'I miss you. I have to rush, but I will try to call you this weekend. Love you.'

After a few weeks, I had already created my routine, and

## VERONICA LLORCA-SMITH

Taipei started to feel familiar. I often thought of my friends back in Spain, working for law firms doing a nine-to-five; I didn't envy them and the corporate life. Learning about the Chinese culture and language was far more interesting than studying books about law, and the paycheck was more generous too.

One day, during the Chinese culture class, Miss Gu warned us, 'You can't truly understand Chinese culture without understanding *feng shui*.'

She was a big fan of *feng shui* and introduced us to its basics. I listened with fascination. *Feng shui*, she explained, is all about letting the energy flow. It's not only a philosophy but also a very profitable business. The most reputable *feng shui* masters in China can earn a fortune. Just like some people have life coaches in Western culture, many people in China, particularly wealthy businesspeople and celebrities, have their own *feng shui* master.

*Feng shui* impacts the seating arrangement at dinner, the architecture, how to place furniture in a home, and even the decision to buy a house. Miss Gu was also a big believer in the healing power of jade. That's why she wore multiple green jade bracelets she would never take off, as they were amulets of luck to draw good energy and repel the bad one. From the color of the jade, and depending on whether the green was turning darker or brighter as it was worn, she could tell a lot about her own energy and the energy around her. After my lesson, I bought a green jade bracelet at a local jewelry store and emailed Vicky a picture.

I was always keen to attend Chinese culture lessons. It was the last lesson of the day and a relief after three hours of intensive Mandarin classes. One day, we were doing an activity, and each student had to pick a number. When it was my turn, I chose number four. Mortified, Miss Gu jumped on her seat.

'We never pick number four in China because it's unlucky,' she said. 'It's pronounced "Si", which sounds similar to death,

## THE FLIGHT HOME

and we believe it brings bad luck.'

After she explained that, I started to notice how the number four was missing from many places, from buildings where they had removed all the floors that ended in four to even street numbers that omitted the number four. On the other hand, eight is the lucky number. It's pronounced "Ba", which sounds similar to "Fa", the character for wealth, and it's the most coveted number in China for car registration plates, dates for significant events, and lottery tickets.

Most days, I ate dinner in local places and learned that Chinese people could read a person based on how they hold and use chopsticks. Once, a Shanghainese student called Hua complimented me at the dorm's canteen while we were having dinner.

'You hold the chopsticks very high and elegantly. It means you are someone who loves travel and adventure, a world citizen.'

I nodded pleasantly in surprise and said, 'Thank you,' in Chinese with a slight bow.

Going to the night markets in Taipei was one of my favorite hobbies on the weekends. We strolled along the food streets, pecking at the different food and trying to guess what was on each tray. Sometimes we ventured into trying some of the samples. There were BBQ sticks of everything from chicken and shrimp, to insects, and sea cucumbers. I discovered a very stinky type of tofu, appropriately called stinky tofu, but never dared to try it. Every other stand sold bubble milk tea, one of the local specialties in Taipei. It's sweet and tasty and has some jelly bubbles in it. Some booths had long queues with dozens of customers waiting. Many were tourists who had traveled from all over Asia to Taipei for the iconic bubble tea and local treats.

At night, Taipei turned into a party town, with tons of bars and clubs with Western cocktails, and Western music. Fancy people dressed in designer clothes danced to the beeps of outlandish DJs who wore sunglasses to look even cooler and drank cans of Redbull. There were very few Western females. Seeing any in town was rare except for a few students. However, there were quite a few Western guys in their 20s and 30s, particularly Canadians and Americans. Many were English teachers hired by international schools; others had come for an adventure, to learn Chinese, or travel around Asia. Mixed couples of Western guys with local Taiwanese girls were common, but I never saw a Western female with an Asian man while I was there.

One day, as I was washing my hands in the bathroom of the fancy nightclub, Roxy, a Taiwanese girl, looked at me and said with an amiable smile, 'You look Latina. Are you Spanish?'

I said, 'Yes,' and we started speaking a mix of English and Chinese. Her name was Fairy, and she was from Taipei. She had spent a summer in Barcelona learning a bit of Spanish. She was petite, had a cute little face, and everything in her was highly curated, from her hair to her toes and porcelain skin. She couldn't have picked a more suitable English name.

At the end of the night, she handed me a napkin and whispered in my ear, in between the beeps from the techno music, 'This is my number. Call me, and I will show you the best of Taipei.'

Fairy became my weekend party buddy. She had a different Louis Vuitton bag and a pair of earrings for every occasion. Her dad was a wealthy businessman, and she lived in a villa in Taipei with her fluffy, equally manicured cat, Peach. I tried to understand what she did for a living multiple times and eventually concluded that she didn't do anything. She was the equivalent of a Beverly Hills socialite or an Instagram celebrity, except there was no social media at the time. Her hobby was to go out, have dinner in fancy restaurants and make sure she didn't miss the best parties in town. I was up for that, and that's

## THE FLIGHT HOME

precisely what we did every single weekend for the entire time I was in Taipei. She would come and pick me up in her fancy white BWM at the dorm, and off we went, ready to party all night and give it all on the dance floor.

'We are like the Asian version of Thelma and Louise,' I told her once, joking, as she collected me up on a Saturday night.

Before I realized it, it was time to say goodbye to Taipei. The three months of studying and partying ended, but the Asian adventure continued. On the last day of school, Miss Gu prepared local sweets made with red beans and Chinese tea.

She pointed at a wooden tray with a tea set inside and joyfully announced, 'Today, I will show you how you drink tea in China.'

She had two teapots, one with *pu'er* tea and the other with hot water. She poured the tea into a cup and then topped it with hot water. She asked me to fill hers, and as I did, she gently knocked on the wooden table with her finger knuckles. I stared at her, surprised.

'This gesture with your fingers symbolizes the movement of bowing to say thank you and show gratitude. It's a tradition from the old days when the subjects bowed before the Emperor as part of the dining etiquette.' Since that day, I started doing the table bow with my fingers, to the awe of many Chinese.

By December 2003, it was time to prepare for my next destination, Shanghai. Work at the Spanish Trade Commission in Shanghai began in early January, and I had ten days off for Christmas and New Year. I organized a trip to Thailand with other interns, and we went backpacking.

I wasn't interested in fancy international hotels with Western-style buffets. I wanted backpackers hostels, dorm rooms, public transport, street walking, and street food. I wanted to breathe the culture, enjoy the smells of the food markets, and discover the real Thailand and the way locals live.

## VERONICA LLORCA-SMITH

'This is pure chaos,' I said as we left the airport in an improvised tuk-tuk. Taipei had motorbikes and scooters everywhere, but Bangkok was a jungle. The drivers didn't wear helmets, no one respected the traffic lights, everyone was honking, and the average number of passengers on a scooter was 2.5, as many had two adults and a child squeezed in between without a helmet.

'How can they be smiling when death is around the corner?' asked Javier sarcastically.

I replied with nervous laughter, 'I have no idea, but I'm not dying in a tuk-tuk. Let's take a normal taxi next time.'

Our tuk-tuk driver was an expert at ignoring red lights too.

'Sir, Sir, careful, please!' I begged from behind.

He ignored me and occasionally yelled something back with a toothless smile while pressing his foot on the accelerator, like a maniac. I closed my eyes and clenched my fists at every intersection or red light. My strategy worked, and we made it safe and sound to the city center, the busy district of Sukhumvit. I handed him some Baht banknotes feeling nauseous and relieved.

As we started to walk along the street toward our backpackers hostel, I noticed the different features between Thai and Chinese, the different skin complexion and eye shape. We left our bags at reception and ventured into the neighborhood.

'Let's try this place, the food looks fresh, and I'm starving!' I said, pointing at a small restaurant on the corner.

We ordered chicken satay, pad Thai, coconut curry, and thom kha gai soup, randomly pointing at the pictures on the plastic menu. The food arrived promptly, and it was delicious. I could taste exotic ingredients like coconut oil, local herbs, and chili. Suddenly I started to feel hot everywhere. My mouth was on fire. The waiter was a young skinny guy with a cheeky smile.

He stared at me, covering his mouth behind his hand, and said with a flirting smile, 'Spicy is good for you. Makes you

## THE FLIGHT HOME

pretty, like Pretty Woman.'

I finished my soup, although I wasn't looking any prettier by the end. I was sweating and couldn't feel my mouth from the chili. The others were laughing while tears were rolling down my cheek.

The next few days, we explored every corner of Bangkok, from massage parlors where petite Thai women gave us deep tissue Thai massages to the famous Chatuchak Market, the largest in Thailand. Besides the street markets and the delicious and spicy Thai food, I looked forward to discovering the Thai lifestyle. Bangkok is known as Asia's party town, the hot place for bachelors parties and girls weekends.

We first walked along a famous street where we could buy anything, as long as it was fake: fake Louis Vuitton bags, fake Gucci, fake Rolex, fake Nike, fake, fake, fake. What struck me the most was a neat booth where we could fake any document to pretend to be anyone. The most popular item was a fake international drivers license that allowed driving in most countries. I picked a dummy one and suspiciously inspected it, wondering who would dare to drive in this place after my life-and-death experience with the tuk-tuk driver. We then went to the hot club called Bed, which all the backpackers raved about at the hostel. It was a glamorous nightclub with square beds covered in white linen sheets. Gorgeous Thai staff dressed in sensual white outfits served colorful cocktails and bottles of champagne. We danced, partied until dawn, and saw the sunrise as we returned to the hostel.

Bangkok had two faces — the colorful, vibrant city that radiated energy from every corner during the day and a very dark side at night. Old white men held hands with very young local girls and sometimes boys. Many were not much older than I was when I started university at seventeen, which gave me a bitter taste. No one blinked an eye, and I felt helpless looking at their robotic smiles.

After the stopover in Bangkok, we took a domestic flight to the city of Chiang Mai, in northern Thailand, famous for its landscape and Buddhist temples, considered amongst the most beautiful in Asia. The town was rural and well-preserved, as it hadn't become a big tourist destination as yet. With a map of the town, and my camera, I rented an old purple bike that was slightly rusty and embarked on a mission to discover the countryside. The list of temples was endless, and I ticked them off the map and took pictures as I went. The Buddhist monks were barefoot, covered in bright orange tunics, and were all accurate replicas of each other. Thin bodies, with dark skin and shaved heads, they walked around graciously, with a soft chanting and a consistent hum in the background. The temples smelled like incense and were predominantly gold and red. Most of them had silver trays with offerings to Buddha, from fruit and candies to fake bank notes representing wealth. I thought of my grandma in the Canary Islands and the many colors of her faith. In Thailand, Faith wore orange.

One of the monks allowed me to visit his humble home. A small room in a wooden cabin with the bare minimum of a bed, a small wooden bedside table, and a couple of shelves with dozens of books about Buddha. I couldn't understand anything, as the Thai alphabet is a total enigma in the eyes of a foreigner, with its delicate calligraphy where round characters elegantly connect, forming a wave of words.

'Home, sweet home,' he said in his broken English with a charming smile, pointing at the small room as if he was showing me a palace.

'It's beautiful,' I said with gratitude and a gentle bow replicating his.

## THE FLIGHT HOME

When New Year came, I was excited to celebrate my first New Year's Eve in a new country and continent and was ready to bring in 2004 in style. I had experienced New Year's in many different places around the world. Regardless of the different traditions, like dressing in white in Brazil or eating twelve grapes at midnight in Spain, the festive spirit was always the same. Everyone was happy to start a new year, to make a new wish, to hope for a better world, and to join the gym and lose the extra pounds. We had dinner in one of the local street restaurants with a big terrace outside, and when midnight came, we raised our champagne glasses to celebrate the year 223 in the Thai calendar. That's when I discovered that Thai people have their own calendar, and I realized I would have to unlearn many things to understand this new world. I thought of Vicky and Mom, who were still in the year 222 in Spain.

The Thailand experience only lasted ten days. Back at Bangkok Airport, I was about to exchange my Thai Baht for US dollars but decided to keep them in my wallet at the last minute. *I will be back*, I thought to myself. Exactly a year later, in December 2004, I went back to Thailand, this time to the south, to visit the famous Phi Phi islands where Leonardo di Caprio was featured in the movie, *The Beach*. The water was pristine; the island had exuberant nature and coconut trees.

'It's just like the movie,' I exclaimed as I took a picture from the wooden boat.

I returned to the Canary Islands two days later to spend Christmas with Mom and Vicky in Fuerteventura. On the 26$^{th}$ of December, we were watching TV at home when suddenly, they broadcasted the footage of the Phi Phi islands on the national news. I turned up the volume but couldn't recognize anything on the screen. There were ruins, havoc, and debris everywhere; streets were turned into improvised rivers, pulling trees, and cars with the strength of the current. Thai mothers desperately sought their children, and people cried in agony.

The TV presenter kept on repeating the word tsunami. Most resorts and shops in Ko Phi Phi, where we had stayed, were single-floor constructions very close to the sea, and many of them were now gone. The beach resort where we slept, the scuba diving shop, and the ice cream place had vanished entirely. It was as if a little piece of Earth had just been swiped away to somewhere in the ocean. The 2004 tsunami devastated hundreds of kilometers of beaches and coastline in South-East Asia and killed 227,000 people. I escaped the tsunami by two days, forty-eight hours. Others weren't as lucky.

On January 14$^{th}$, 2004, I landed at Shanghai Pudong International Airport. I was entering a communist country where I didn't know anyone. There was no free press, access to international newspapers, or credit cards. I had goosebumps when I read the sign at immigration that said, "Welcome to the People's Republic of China".

I took a deep breath as I looked at that sign telling myself, 'You got this.'

My first impression of Shanghai was a big, cold, grey city spread across a never-ending area. The drive from the airport to the city center took over an hour and passed hundreds of identical high-rise buildings. It was a vertical city as much as it was a horizontal one. In 2004, Shanghai had just over twenty million inhabitants, half of Spain's population.

Unlike Taipei, Shanghai did not feel welcoming when I arrived. Whereas in Taipei, people looked at me with friendly smiles and were often willing to help me with directions, Chinese people seemed were puzzled and suspicious of foreigners. I tried at first to ask for help from random strangers on the street using my basic Chinese, but they frequently crossed their arms

## THE FLIGHT HOME

anxiously and walked in the opposite direction, staring back. Some, especially those with little children, would point at me and laugh, occasionally taking pictures.

Chinese have a casual name to refer to foreigners: *lao wai*. They also think Westerners have big noses. Over time I became used to their curious looks, with fingers pointing at our big noses, and unsolicited attention from strangers. Although there were a few foreigners in Shanghai in 2004, the numbers were still small, and most tended to hang out in expat-friendly places such as the French Concession, luxury hotels, and international shopping malls like West Gate Mall.

Settling into Shanghai was an ordeal, therefore, every little win was rewarding. There was no Google, so we had to rely on our street intuition to find our way, and the weather was freezing. I had been working from day one, so I only had one hour after work to try my luck in finding my Shanghai home. One day I walked along Beijing Road after work and randomly picked one of the many real estate offices that were located side-by-side. My agent, Chen, didn't speak a word of English, but he always smiled back with, 'OK, OK,' and a thumbs-up. Luckily, I hadn't skipped the lesson about houses and furniture with Miss Gu in Taipei.

My basic Chinese was enough to explain to him that I wanted a flat with one bedroom, one kitchen, and one bathroom and that my budget was 3,500RMB per month, equivalent to $400 US at the time. I also wanted it near the office so I could walk to work in the morning. I didn't know enough Chinese to tell him I preferred a quiet place with Western decorations and a heater, so I ended up in a tiny flat on the $67^{th}$ floor of an old Chinese building. It was not quite what I had envisaged, but it was all my broken Chinese could afford me.

The flat was old inside, with outdated furniture. The 80s

flower-patterned curtains looked old-fashioned but the views were nice, and it was close enough to the office. Once I agreed to take the flat, I had to sign a contract in Chinese without the benefit of an English version. I had only learned to speak Chinese and hadn't studied Chinese characters, so I could have ended up signing a marriage contract with agent Chen, as I had no idea what all those characters meant. I trusted him as he enthusiastically gave me the thumbs-up, and luckily it was a rental agreement. Over time I became used to signing paperwork in Chinese without knowing what it meant. I signed forms at hotels, letters from couriers, and police declarations in Chinese, and no one seemed to bother the least. Chinese are very good at bureaucracy and following instructions, so it was all good, as long as the paperwork was signed.

I moved in the next day. The first night the temperature outside was a windy -2C Celsius, and I could feel the cold filtering through the windows. I tucked myself under the blanket and resented Miss Gu for not teaching us the word "heater" in Chinese.

Walking into the Spanish Trade Commission for the first time, I discovered my new office in the luxurious Mei Long Zhen Shopping Mall on Nanjing West Road. I carefully selected a white blouse and a pair of black pants for my first day at work and felt proud of myself looking in the mirror in the elevator as I pressed button number 25. All the interns were sitting together in an open area at the back of the office, and I was assigned a desk near the window, where I had views of the entire city. Javier was sitting just next to me.

I looked at the view and told him, 'I can't believe we get paid to work here. Look at those vistas.'

Once I had my flat and started working, I enrolled at a gym nearby; my day-to-day life was not much different from any

## THE FLIGHT HOME

twenty-three-year-old in Europe. I worked in a friendly office, had coffee with the other interns while gossiping in the pantry, and looked forward to the weekend to party, and the next pay cheque, to plan the next holiday.

Although Shanghai started to become more international, it remained a vast Chinese city with few urban areas and compounds dedicated to foreigners. There was only one authentic Italian restaurant in town called, Damarco. It was owned by a big man from Naples called Marco, who made delicious thin-crust pizza and was always boisterous. I was there every Thursday, and he always called me *Bella* and gave me a complimentary glass of prosecco.

There were only a few clubs where we could dance and drink at night, including Park 97 and Zapatas; however, every week in 2005, nightclubs started to pop up everywhere, like mushrooms. More and more companies began to see Shanghai as the gateway to China. Big clubs, restaurant franchises, and bars opened monthly, with extravagant parties and Russian models at the door. As a white girl, I was immediately given VIP status and was invited to the fanciest places and clubs. Having international faces automatically gave the venue coveted international status.

In 2005, the iconic Bar Rouge opened on The Bund, the famous avenue facing the Huangpu River overlooking Pudong, the eastern side of the city. Bar Rouge was always featured in the *Time Out Shanghai* magazine for expats and immediately became an epic destination for any tourist, cool crowd, and local fashionistas. It was located in the best spot, had fancy European DJs, and offered the best cocktails made by handsome French waiters who set the bar on fire with alcohol. There were gorgeous East European models at the entrance, and I felt like I was in a fashionable club in New York or Paris, but this was Shanghai. I was there every weekend and felt like my life was on fire, just like the bar.

My boss Rachel assigned me my main project at work. I had to write a comprehensive report about the fashion industry in China. It required a holistic analysis of the Chinese market, distribution channels, consumer trends, prices, competition, key fairs, and trade shows. Hesitantly, she warned me that few resources were available as there were no search engines in China.

'It's a bit like the wild west here, except everybody is Chinese,' she said.

'Don't worry, I will figure it out, and it will be a brilliant opportunity to improve my Chinese,' I replied confidently.

I had no idea where to start, but it didn't matter. I knew it was a golden opportunity to learn the ins-and-outs of an exploding market that most Westerners knew little about. I started researching, reading, and consuming any information that could add value to my project.

I also had a small budget for my research that allowed me to travel to the neighboring cities in the Zhejiang province and visit fashion trade shows, suppliers, and distributors. Every other week I took a local train to discover a new city, from Wenzhou, the city of leather, to Datang, the town of socks, and Suzhou, the silk capital. Most were unheard of outside of China, yet they were each home to a few million inhabitants. The scale of people in China was a different beast to any I had experienced before.

My project kept me busy at work, and my Chinese developed as fast as the pages in my report. I called import agents daily, talked to distributors in Chinese on the phone, visited department stores, and asked questions of shop attendants about their customers. I visited random places in the city to see what Shanghai street fashion was like, attended every fashion fair, and sometimes hosted our booth to welcome Spanish visitors.

## THE FLIGHT HOME

The best part of the job was attending the VIP parties for new brands that were launching in China. The foreign trade commissions and consulates were always invited to attend these events. I became a regular at these glamorous parties, from Armani's opening party to Dolce & Gabbana, and other luxury brand events.

Throughout my research, I also learned random facts, like how Chinese men preferred shoes without shoelaces or how Western brands had to fully customize their collections to be successful with the Chinese consumer. I once entered a local shop to learn about Shanghainese fashion and trends. The shop assistant rushed in my direction and apologetically explained that they had no sizes for bigger girls like me. At the time, I was a standard Western size small, but I was a big girl in China. I decided not to venture into the local shops anymore, and felt a huge sense of relief when ZARA opened stores in China in 2005, and the first one was right in front of my office building.

The year at the Trade Commission went as fast as the Maglev bullet train, the fastest in the world, which connected Shanghai Airport to the city. Every day was intense. I woke up in the morning, headed to the office, spent hours working on my reports, headed back home, and studied Chinese or watched Chinese TV. I had deliberately chosen not to have Internet at home so that my only entertainment options would be in Chinese. Out of boredom, I sometimes studied in the evening. Weekends were all about partying, and on Monday morning, I pressed the repeat button and did it all again.

I published my 100-page fashion report, and every page was written based on my hands-on experience, trips, calls, and meetings. Thanks to my excellent teacher Lee, and many nosy taxi drivers, my Chinese was close to fluent, and my boss started to ask me to join her meetings to help translate the conversation.

When the internship at the Trade Commission was coming to an end, it was time to decide what was next, and all I knew for sure was that I was not ready to leave China just yet. I had only begun to discover the country and was hungry for more.

Few jobs were available for foreigners, as most foreign companies were more interested in sending experienced executives with costly expat packages to China. I didn't have enough experience to apply for those senior roles. The more local entry jobs targeted local Chinese, so there wasn't a sweet spot for someone like me.

Many colleagues decided to go back to Europe after a year. China was too harsh. Others, primarily men, chose to stay and found work placements in Spanish companies interested in investing or selling their products in China. They were all busy interviewing, but I hadn't received a single invite for an interview.

One day, Javier asked out loud in the office, 'Who is going to interview for the logistics company?'

One after the other, the five male interns replied. Most had already secured a job and had declined the interview. I looked around puzzled, and asked with curiosity,

'Which logistics company?'

Everyone looked at me with surprise, until my colleague Abdon said, 'Oops, you should put a male name on your CV next time.'

Everyone started laughing, including me, although I was fuming and annoyed deep inside.

Having focused on fashion for a year, I had no interest in logistics, but I wanted to have a shot at the interview, mainly because I wanted the same opportunity. I found the contact details of the hiring manager and sent him an email after having recomposed it myself.

*Dear Jose,*

## THE FLIGHT HOME

*I heard from our Trade Commissioner that you are looking for a manager for your company in Shanghai, and I'm aware you have started the interview process. I understand you are meeting all the current interns, and I would like to express my interest in the position.*
   *Please let me know when we can meet.*
   *Regards,*
   *Veronica*

Thirty minutes later, I received a friendly invitation to attend an interview that week. I met with Jose in person at a hotel lobby, and a week later, I signed an offer to become the China Manager in Shanghai. The headquarters were in Hong Kong, and I was in charge of kicking off the business in China, obtaining government licenses, and hiring a local team. A few months later, we joked about the interview process. He admitted that management feared that a young Spanish woman would not be tough enough to thrive in a market like China, let alone in a male-dominated industry such as logistics. I was the first woman to run a Spanish logistics company in China, and we were the first Spanish freight forwarding company to obtain a government license to operate in the country.

I started my new job in January 2005 and became used to being the only woman in the room. I was the only woman amongst the other foreign freight forwarders in Shanghai, who were primarily European and North American white men. I was the only woman at the international company meetings in Spain with all the other regional directors; most were twice my age, and I was the only woman visible in key ports like Tianjin, Qingdao, or Xiamen, when we visited our Chinese agents across the country. The Chinese agents would frequently ask where my boss was when they first met me in person, but once

I started speaking Chinese, it would reset the tone and level up the playing field. Most foreigners I met couldn't speak Chinese, except for a basic conversational level, so the language became my superpower and allowed me to open many doors.

I loved my job, but the corridor jokes and comments about me being a woman was a constant. The expressions varied from, 'Have you found a boyfriend yet?' to 'Are you going to get married soon?', 'You are overcooking the rice,' a Spanish expression for growing too old, or 'Tic-tock, your clock is ticking.'

I always brushed these comments off with a gracious smile. I was twenty-five and had no intention of marrying or having children anytime soon, but apparently, it was not the norm for women to stay single, and it always made for a good joke. It never upset me or got under my skin, which was pretty thick by then, but I never heard the same jokes about my male counterparts, who were labelled golden bachelors while my rice was overcooked in the oven.

After three years in Shanghai, my nomadic voice awakened, calling for the next destination, and the screams were getting louder. I had already accomplished my primary mission of learning Chinese and had taken the logistics business from its infancy to a more mature stage, with offices in different cities nationwide.

In the space of three years, I visited all the iconic landmarks in China from the magnificent Great Wall in Beijing, to the Terracotta Warriors in Xian. I saw the beautiful Hainan island, the Hawaii of China; Suzhou, the Venice of China; the Yellow Mountains; Nanjing, the old capital; Yiwu, the city of the one-dollar items; the Guilin mountains, which featured in the 100 Chinese Yuan banknotes; Chengdu, the town of the Pandas, and every major port city.

The furthest west I went in China was Xinjiang, a vast territory

## THE FLIGHT HOME

of primarily deserts and mountains in the northwest. Xinjiang intrigued me because of the ancient Silk Road that passed through it. The population of Xinjiang is mainly Turkic Uyghur, a minority very different from the Han ethnic majority in China. Their skin complexion is darker, and their features are less Asian. In Xinjiang, I met for the first time Chinese people who were Muslim and whose culture resembled Arabic, with its spicy food and kebabs, street markets, colorful outfits, and turbans. The city had a fragrance of spices like cumin and cinnamon and smelled like a bazaar of antiques. The locals spoke Mandarin fluently but with a strong accent, as their primary language is Uyghur, a Turkic language similar to Uzbek but written in Arabic script. Very little of China was recognizable in Xinjiang except for their skill at the market bargaining game. Because of my olive skin and Mandarin accent, some Han Chinese occasionally asked me whether I was from Xinjiang.

My passion for traveling knew no borders, and I took every opportunity to discover Asia, by traveling every Lunar New Year, Golden Week, and Mid-Autumn Festival. I visited the famous Shibuya crossing in Tokyo, went snorkeling on the island of Borneo, visited Lombok in Indonesia, and even traveled to India to visit the Taj Mahal, making a treasured dream come true.

By the time I received my annual bonus in December 2006, I had saved over 20,000 Euros and decided to make my first investment. I talked to a bank manager in Spain, and they granted me a mortgage to purchase my first flat, a small duplex in Tenerife. As I was processing the paperwork, I had to explain where the funds for the deposit came from. I read the different options: capital gains, savings, donation, and inheritance. I paused, looking at the Yuyuan Gardens through the window of my office. So much had happened since I had left Spain.

I ticked the box of "personal savings" and signed the form

with a proud smile, knowing that deep down, it was all thanks to the inheritance I had received in the currency of education and languages.

The next day my company offered me a promotion to move to Asia's World City, Hong Kong.

## Chapter Eight
## Becoming an Ironwoman – Fulfilment

'What happens if I don't like Hong Kong or the job?' I asked Arturo, the company's CEO, as we were having dinner in a French restaurant in Shanghai to discuss my future.

'Well,' he replied, adjusting his thick glasses and looking into my eyes, 'we both know what will happen. You will leave, you will find something that you love doing, and you will keep growing. That's why we hired you.'

I chuckled. He was right.

'Have you found a boyfriend yet, by the way?' he asked, teasing me. I shook my head sideways and started laughing.

'Not yet. You got married at sixty-two. Ask me in thirty-five years. Free as a bird.'

We both laughed and cheered with a glass of Moët & Chandon. I signed the contract in the morning and started preparing for my departure.

I landed in Hong Kong in April 2007. Hong Kong was country number eight in the book of my life, and eight being the lucky number in China, it was a good omen. I had previously visited the city multiple times for work, and it had always given me the impression of a giant concrete jungle with a lot of urban life and noise and little nature. On the day I arrived, I went for a stroll on the street. It was hot and humid, with a heavy haze in the air, and the Hong Kong Observatory app indicated 95 percent humidity. I wandered around my new neighborhood, Mid-Levels, trying to become familiar with a place that was once again home, although everything smelled different here.

I looked up and around, the city continued to surprise me with its blatant contrasts, its ultra-modern skyscrapers next to rundown Chinese mom-and-pop shops. Maseratis and Porches were driven by chauffeurs next to old Chinese men pulling heavy wooden carts with newspapers; an elegant beauty salon and a Louis Vuitton store across from a local herbal tea shop. I walked along the fruit market on Gaugh Street and stopped at one booth to purchase a bag of mangos from the Philippines and some lychees which looked juicy and delicious. When it was my turn, the old lady smiled and uttered a few words in Cantonese as she weighed the fruits on an old scale. I didn't understand, handed her a note of one hundred Hong Kong dollars, and thanked her in Mandarin while she prepared the change. It was in that moment, I decided I wanted to learn Cantonese.

'So, how is Hong Kong?' Vicky asked curiously as she picked up the phone.

She was now living and working in Fuerteventura as a French teacher. I looked at the views of the city from the window of my new flat on the 27th floor of Center Stage on Hollywood Road.

'I'm loving it,' I replied. 'It's like the New York of Asia. Hong Kong is very cosmopolitan, and everyone speaks English. Things are much easier here than in China, and my flat is small but beautiful. The building even has a pool and a spa. I hope you can come and visit.'

Soon after I arrived, I made an Argentinian friend, Virginia, who invited me to join a junk boat on the weekend.

'A junk boat?' I asked curiously, as I had never heard that

## THE FLIGHT HOME

word before.

'Yes, it's a traditional Chinese wooden boat. There are around twenty-five people, and we all bring food, drink, and music. It takes us to Sai Kung, and the beaches there look just like Thailand. You won't believe it.'

On Sunday, I met the group on Pier Number 9 in Central at 10:00 a.m. and jumped onto my first junk boat. I introduced myself to the guys and girls around me. It was a mix of Europeans, South Americans, and a few Asians. In fifteen minutes, I joined conversations in five different languages. They were all young, single, and living in Hong Kong as expats. The boat took off, and we arrived in Tai Long Wan an hour-and-a-half later. I stared at the beach as we approached the coast, pulled my iPhone out of my bag, and exclaimed in awe as I took a picture,

'This is stunning. I never expected to see beaches like this in Hong Kong, with golden sand and pristine water.'

Jose, a Spanish guy sitting next to me, nodded and added, 'Wait until you start hiking and see the monkeys, the views from the peaks, and the wild pigs. You can even go camping here but be careful with the snakes.'

The day was a long party with people swimming, dancing, and tanning on the boat. Some of us went swimming to the beach and sat on the warm sand with the cool waves splashing our feet. As we returned to the city in the afternoon, we all rushed to the front of the junk boat and took a picture with Hong Kong's skyline in the background, the sun setting, and everybody smiling. It was only my first weekend, and I had already fallen in love with Hong Kong.

In June, I celebrated my 27$^{th}$ birthday and threw a beach party on Deep Water Bay, in Hong Kong Island, with a Brazilian friend called Mauro. He was from Rio and had his birthday a few days before me. We dressed in white, decorated the beach with white candles and flowers, and had over thirty friends join us.

'Just like Rio,' Mauro said, hugging me as everyone sang happy birthday in different languages.

Hong Kong was the perfect spot to continue my backpacking expedition across South-East Asia and explore the continent. I purchased a world map on the street market, hung it in the living room and kept crossing off destinations with a red marker.

First, I went hiking in the Sapa mountains, in the countryside of Vietnam, and slept in a local family's hut. Then, I visited the Perhentian islands in Malaysia.

In December 2007, I knocked on the door of Arturo's office.

'Come in,' he said as he checked his Blackberry with a severe expression. 'Have a seat. What's up?'

I sat before him, took a deep breath, and explained that I wanted to resign. I was clear and assertive, like I had rehearsed in front of the mirror at home.

'I always knew that this moment would arrive sooner or later. Is it about the money? Does your offer pay you more?'

I shook my head. 'It's not about the money. I love working here and the team but I've done my time in logistics. I'm ready to move on and learn something new. It's been three amazing years, but I want to learn something new.'

'Are you going to the competitors?' he asked suspiciously, raising his grey eyebrows.

'No,' I answered without hesitation. 'I'm going to a different industry, of skin care. I don't want money; I want a challenge.'

My throat was dry, and my body was tense, despite trying to look composed. Arturo put his glasses on the table and suddenly relaxed.

He said jokingly in his hoarse voice, 'I will let you go, but only because you are not going to the competitors. I'm sure those bastards will try to hire you the moment they hear you are not

# THE FLIGHT HOME

with us anymore. Learn, travel, and live your life. I would have done the same.'

He hugged me as I was leaving; I turned around and said two words as I was closing the door,

'Thank you.'

I didn't tell him, but the new job paid significantly less. I had to leave the fancy flat the company provided, and no longer had an expat contract. However, I didn't care about the money, provided it was enough to allow me to travel and discover Asia. I was hungry to learn, to work in a different industry, and to have the freedom to do business anywhere, from Australia to Japan and Cambodia.

I started working for the new company, GTS Group, in 2008, and the nomadic life began. I had a small carry-on suitcase that was always ready with the basics: toiletries, chargers, a wallet with coins and banknotes from different countries, and my passport. One week I was visiting distributors in Vietnam, the next, I was presenting to our clients at the Grand Hyatt in Taipei or visiting spas and doing market research in Bangkok. Every three months, I flew to Bergamo in Italy to meet with the executive team and report on the progress in Asia. My boss Silvia was a lovely woman, half-Argentinian, half-Italian. She had big brown eyes, short curly hair, and a warm smile that filled the room.

When she interviewed me in Hong Kong with the HR Director, she told me in Italian, 'You are exactly what we are looking for. We need someone with the energy, drive, and curiosity to go and figure things out in Asia solo. Speaking Italian and Chinese is just the icing on the cake. *Brava, bravissima,*' she added, enthusiastically shaking her hands the Italian way while the HR Director, Rodolfo, inspected me with a serious demeanor from the corner of his eyes.

Work hard and play hard was the title of my new life, and there was no pause button in it. Hong Kong always had something exciting, from rooftop parties to the Rugby Sevens sports events, junk boats, and club openings on Wyndham Street. I continued taking Mandarin lessons, signed up for a gym, and started running with my German friend Edith on the weekends, on Bowen Road, overlooking the entire city. Facebook was becoming mainstream, and every week I posted pictures from trips around Asia or parties in Hong Kong.

In my free time, I searched for exotic destinations most people had never visited. I explored the temples in Angkor Wat in Cambodia, the stunning pagodas in Myanmar, and snorkeled in Borneo. Back in Spain, my university friends were starting to marry, have children, and buy mortgaged houses in the suburbs while I was busy ticking off new destinations on my world map at home.

In 2008, I returned to Spain to attend the wedding of Diana, my friend from university in her village, Plasencia, in the South of Spain. It was the first time I reunited with all my classmates from Salamanca after we had graduated in 2002.

'You have become Chinese,' my friend Tamara said as she saw me. 'You even look a bit Chinese now.'

I hugged her, and we sat together at the church as Diana walked down the aisle in a beautiful white gown and a long trail. We all drank, shared stories, and danced until dawn.

'Where do you think you will settle down?' Maria asked me when we were having dinner.

I frowned, thinking about the eight countries I had lived in, and replied, 'I don't know. I don't think I will ever settle down.' The friends at the table started laughing, thinking it was a joke, but it wasn't. I didn't know what settling down meant.

Compared to China, Hong Kong was free and international

## THE FLIGHT HOME

expats were everywhere. I could easily access Google and Facebook, travel in and out, and do everything in record efficiency, from opening a bank account to renting a flat, or exchanging foreign currency. I could also pay for anything with a colorful card called Octopus, where I recharged money, and could use it to buy groceries, pay utility bills at the 7/11, and even settle payments in public hospitals. Hong Kong offered the best of both the West and the East. There were opportunities everywhere if I kept my eyes open, my mind curious, and if I was at the right place and time.

After living in the city for a few years, it was time for a change. I wanted something big, a challenge, a new country, a new project. I didn't know what I was looking for, but my sixth sense warned me it was time for a fresh start.

And that's precisely what happened on the 5th of October 2011, as I walked through the luxurious IFC Mall in the Central District to visit a customer's office. I was passing along the shops and noticed that the Apple Store was preparing for its grand opening. Everyone was talking about it in town. It would be the first Apple Store in Hong Kong and promised to become one of the city's iconic landmarks, as it had a premium location and the best views over Victoria Harbour. The store was breathtaking.

Steve Jobs sadly passed away that day after his long fight against cancer, and it was all over the news. I stopped by to take pictures of the beautiful facade and the many handwritten letters, post-its, and flower bouquets that local fans and tourists had dropped at the front of the store as a tribute to Steve. I had always admired him, his philosophy, and what he had been able to create, starting from his little garage in California. I read every single post-it and stopped in front of one.

It read, 'You can't connect the dots looking forward. You can only connect the dots looking backward. So you must trust that the dots will somehow connect in your future.' I kept staring at that yellow note, thinking of the dots in my life across the different continents and wondering how they were all connected.

I kept gazing through the tall glass windows, trying to sneak a peek into the store, as this was the first time I had seen an Apple Store. It looked majestic and refined, every detail had been meticulously curated, from the display of the products on the tables to the aluminum staircase in the middle. My dream is to work for a company like this, I thought.

I noticed a group of three men and one woman standing in a circle by the door, chatting and pointing at the store. They all had badges with the Apple logo, and I could tell they were management by the confidence they emanated and their assertive body language. As I moved closer, I recognized the woman, Cristina. She was also Spanish, and I had met her many times before through friends at parties, junk boats, and networking events. She was always bubbly and full of energy.

I approached the group, stopped by to say, 'Hi,' and congratulated her on her new job, as I knew she had just joined Apple. We started a casual chat, and I spontaneously said, 'Wow, what an amazing company. It must be incredible to work at Apple.'

Not having any background in technology, I never thought Apple would be a company that could be interested in someone like me. However, as soon as I said those words, she looked at me as if she had just connected two cables and replied, opening her arms, 'You should totally come and work here. You speak languages, are multicultural, and have been in China for years. You would be perfect as a Business Manager. Let me introduce you to the hiring team.'

Before I could react, she introduced me to her colleagues. They were all big men from the US and Australia. Everyone was

## THE FLIGHT HOME

friendly and relaxed, and five minutes later, I was invited for an interview. It sounded too good to be true.

A week later, the interview process began, and I still had no clue what a Business Manager at Apple was. The same three Apple guys were now welcoming me into the office in IFC Mall, but they were sitting down this time. It didn't feel like an interview, as it was an informal conversation. They seemed genuinely interested in knowing more about me and my experience working in Asia and developing businesses from the ground up.

'I have to be honest. I'm not a tech person. I want to make sure you know,' I said awkwardly out of the blue.

Danny, the General Manager, leaned forward on his chair and replied with a thick Australian accent and a confident smile, 'Look, at Apple, we have the best products in the world because we have the best engineers and developers. We are not looking for more technical people. We want people who can inspire teams, who understand the Chinese culture, and who can connect. We are not looking for managers; we want leaders, the best people leaders, and I can see you have that in you.'

The process was long, it took five interviews and six months to receive the offer letter in writing, but on March $3^{rd}$, 2012, I was finally wearing my Apple badge and entered the mysterious Apple world as an employee. On the first day of work, I left the office with a proud grin. I was an Apple leader, and I had earned my badge.

'Veronica, do you need a visa to travel to Australia? We will send you to Sydney and Melbourne for four weeks for your onboarding,' Danny said on my second week.

'Australia?' I replied, ecstatic. 'I will apply for the visa right now.'

A few days later, I was on a flight to Sydney, ready to discover behind-the-scenes Apple. That week, I wrote a LinkedIn post about my new role as a Business Manager, with a picture of a silver Apple logo. I immediately received dozens of messages from old friends and strangers congratulating me and asking for tips for an interview. Recruiters started poking me, and vendors of random products, from software to raw materials, tried to pitch to me every day. I felt like a million-dollar girl.

My onboarding continued, and in July, I flew to the San Francisco. I first spent three weeks on the Apple campus in Cupertino, California, with other Business Managers from the US. I was the youngest one and the only foreigner. The last week I flew to New York to shadow the Business Team at the Apple Store on $5^{th}$ Avenue. I was working for the best company in the world in its number one flagship store, The Cube, the only Apple Store open 24/7.

'It's the most photographed landmark in New York,' my colleague Ricky told me proudly,'even more than the Statue of Liberty.'

The Apple campus in Cupertino had a university vibe and was as multicultural as the European School in Holland. It was modern and beautiful, with see-through glass doors and a lovely grass area with trees and tables for people to relax during the breaks on sunny days. The Apple cafeteria had a rich selection of food from around the world, from Mexican tacos, Italian pizza, salad, curries, sushi, and desserts. Everything was freshly made and smelled delicious, and the staff was friendly and warm.

On my last day at the campus, there was a social event in the afternoon, and all employees were invited to gather outside. There were booths with food and drinks, and a music band was preparing to perform. I looked at the stage as one of the employees walked toward the microphone. It was a tall slim guy with grey hair and glasses, wearing jeans, a black polo shirt, and

## THE FLIGHT HOME

sports shoes. He looked casual and unassuming. He confidently picked up the microphone, looked straight into the crowd with a big smile, and said nothing for a few seconds. As soon as he greeted the audience, I recognized the voice and the face. It was Tim Cook. He welcomed everyone and started talking.

'It doesn't matter what your role at Apple is; every day, you have an opportunity to enhance people's lives. Every single one of you,' he said with a decisive tone. And then he paused. There was silence. He shared some words from Steve Jobs and said his office was still on the campus. It remained empty because Steve was irreplaceable.

'He wanted to make a dent in the Universe,' he added, referring to Steve's famous quote,'and he did. Look around; all of this is his legacy.'

He pointed toward the building, the trees, and the people. He looked down, took a deep breath, and there was silence. No one said a word. Then suddenly, the clapping began and became louder and didn't stop. I felt goosebumps all over my body.

Back in Hong Kong, Apple became a second home. I loved my team, who were all locals from Hong Kong, and I loved speaking Mandarin with them. I also started taking Cantonese lessons during my lunch break to speak the basics and to connect with my colleagues. When the first market-wide event took place, the General Manager invited me to do a brief introduction about business at Apple.

'How fluent is your Chinese?' he asked. 'Would you be confident doing your speech in Mandarin?'

My stomach shrank, I didn't know what I would talk about, but I said, 'Yes.' The following week, I went on stage in the Shangri La Hotel, where 500 Apple employees gathered for the quarterly event. When it was my turn, I grabbed the microphone and started speaking English. Then I switched to Chinese without warning and continued with my speech. A few seconds later, I heard a few claps and then more, and suddenly, the claps turned into a standing ovation. From left to right, I could see dozens of Chinese colleagues smiling and clapping as if I were one of their own. I did a slight bow, thanking the audience, and continued. I thought of Miss Gu, the cold nights in Shanghai learning Chinese, and the many trips around China. Just like Steve Jobs said, my dots were connecting.

Year after year, Apple offered me new opportunities, and I took every single one of them. I traveled to Tianjin in Northern China to support the opening of a new store, I mentored the Business Team in Tokyo as they reopened the Omotesando store, and I visited New York again when I was promoted to Business Leader. My new role also covered Macau, and I took the one-hour ferry every week to spend the day with the team in the first Apple Store in Macau, at the Galaxy Mall.

Around the same time my Apple journey began, I embarked on a new adventure, this time in sports. In 2010, I decided to join a triathlon club called Tritons. Some friends had recommended it as a great social club to make friends, exercise, and meet handsome guys. I was intimidated at the thought of starting a triathlon, but despite my trepidations, I bought a second-hand bike which I called Pinky, a pair of goggles, and signed up for the club membership. I joined a couple of training sessions and was instantly hooked. Instead of coming home at 5:00 a.m. from partying all night in clubs like Dragon-i and Volar, I was leaving home at 5:30 a.m. with my bike kit and my Lycra outfit and would bump into the people coming home drunk at sunrise.

'Do you think she's on drugs?' I overheard a drunk guy say as I was riding past the bars on Caine Road. This happened every Saturday and Sunday morning, and revelers often looked at me twice, rubbing their eyes to make sure I was a real person on a

## THE FLIGHT HOME

real bike and not an alcohol-induced hallucination.

I started training every day before and after work. Mondays and Wednesdays I ran, Tuesdays and Thursdays I cycled in the morning and swam in the evening, and on the weekend, the club organized long bike rides in Lantau Island and swims in Repulse Bay, on the south side of Hong Kong.

'You look so fit,' my colleague Daphne told me at work one day when we were having the lunch break.

I felt strong, and I was keen to perform better and become faster. During the training sessions, I bonded with other girls who had just joined the club as well. I became very close with Bea from France, Jane from Australia, and Ingrid from Sweden. We spent hours together, training, eating carbs after the session, and planning races.

Little by little, I started to set the bar higher. First, I entered short-distance triathlons in Hong Kong, then competed in the famous Laguna Phuket Triathlon, and slowly but steadily, I built my confidence in the racing scene. I signed up for my first Half-Ironman, consisting of a 1.9 km. swim, 90 km. bike ride, and 21 km. run. I raced on Jeju island in South Korea in July 2011, and came second in my age group.

'You have qualified for the world championships of Half-Ironman,' Jane yelled as the results came out. 'We are going to Vegas, baby,' she added, shaking her hips in a hula hoop movement.

'Vegas? What?'

We had both qualified and started jumping in the air with our sweaty triathlon suits and messy hair from hours of exercising. We hadn't even removed the racing number painted on our forearms and decided to accept the slot and race in Vegas. In September 2011, we both crossed the finish line of the world championships and bought a pink T-shirt that read, 'What happens in Vegas stays in Vegas.'

I loved challenging my body to do things I once thought impossible, only to prove myself wrong and keep pushing my limits. One day, as I was getting changed into my swim gear in the changing room, I overheard the coach, Fenella, mention how many Tritons were competing in the Taiwan Ironman competition. The Ironman is the most iconic triathlon race in the world and entails a 3.8 km. swim, 180 km. bike ride, and a full marathon, 42 km. at the end. The event was born on the Big Island of Kona, in Hawaii, when a group of very keen athletes announced the first "Around the Island Triathlon" in 1978, giving birth to the first Ironman competition. I went to the pool and kept on thinking about the Ironman as I swam the laps.

That night I went home and watched YouTube videos of Ironman races around the world and people crossing the finish line. I only intended to spend five minutes browsing, but one hour later, I was still reading stories and clicking on videos. I expected to see only the fittest humans on Earth completing the race. There were many of them, but there were also people with disabilities, competitors on wheelchairs, and blind runners being pulled by their guides with a rope. I saw a teenage boy with cerebral palsy doing the entire race pulled by his dad. The dad was swimming, pulling a canoe, cycling on a special bike, and running, pushing his son in a wheelchair. The boy never stopped smiling during the entire video, and they both cried when they crossed the finish line. I cried as well. It was the Hoyt father-and-son team, and at that moment, I decided to enter an Ironman.

'An Ironman?' asked my friend Bea while we were at a Christmas dinner party in 2011.

I nodded with a grin lifting my glass of champagne.

'Oh, la la,' she said with her French accent, 'This is happening. We are doing the Ironman in Australia next year.'

## THE FLIGHT HOME

We convinced Jane to join us and a few of the guys from the Tritons Club. Our name was on the starter's list. There was no going back.

I spent the next twelve months training almost every day. I would tick off the fifteen-hour training weeks on top of the demanding job at Apple and socialize on Saturday nights. I was tired but relentless. I had a clear goal and a finish line to cross, and there was no room for failing.

'You already are an ironwoman,' Danny told me when I applied for leave at work, 'I have no doubt you are going to cross that finish line. Your level of discipline is incredible.'

On December 16th, 2012, Bea, Jane, and I were together in our long black wetsuit at the beginning of the Ironman swim, having a last good-luck hug. The waves in the jetty of Busselton, in Western Australia looked huge from where we were standing on the beach, and I didn't want to think of the sharks. My heart was racing, and the race gun went off. Hundreds of competitors sprinted into the water. I felt kicks and arms pushing me down and waves crashing in my face, pushing me back to the shore. I swallowed water, but it didn't matter. I was chasing my dream, one stroke at a time.

After the swim, I spotted Bea and Jane on the road once I jumped on the bike. The boys from the club, Dave and Jess, were there as well. Everyone was suffering and fighting their demons but every step took us closer to the finish line. After six hours and thirty minutes on the bike, I changed into my running shoes to start the 42 km. ahead. My legs were stiff and felt like jelly at the same time. It was 1:00 p.m., and the Australian sun had no mercy. There was no shade. The run was four loops, with hundreds of spectators cheering, volunteers handing water and sports drinks, and people playing music.

'Keep it up, Veronica, looking great, mate,' spectators yelled as they saw me running with my name on my bib. The first loop was fun and exciting, I was still fresh and had a solid pace. By the time the fourth loop started, I was swearing in six languages and wondering who had had that terrible idea. Of course, it was me. *One more step, one more step*, I kept telling myself as I shook my hand to shake off the flies that were lying on my sweaty skin. I looked around and saw fit guys sitting sunburnt on the floor, others were shuffling in pain. Many looked like zombies. The ambulance kept collecting competitors who had collapsed due to heatstroke. A sign on the racecourse indicated 22 km. to go. I was exhausted. I stopped at a water station and grabbed my eighth energy gel. It was coffee flavor. I had been going for over nine hours, and the sun was starting to set. It was so close yet so far. *How many more steps?* I kept thinking.

I started shuffling and saw Dave running in the opposite direction. He was struggling, too, but he seemed focused. He was twenty minutes ahead of me.

'You are an ironwoman, 20 km. to go,' he said, with a thumbs-up and a charming smile. The finish line was there, waiting for me. One step at a time, one step at a time, I kept telling myself ...

It was the final stretch. I stared at the digital screen in front of me, I only had 100 meters to go, and suddenly I forgot about the pain, the sore knee, and the exhaustion. I started sprinting, high-fiving the spectators on the other side of the fence. I ran on the red carpet, and as I looked up, I saw my name on the screen: Veronica Llorca—Spain—12 hrs. 41 min. I crossed the finish line among the claps with tears as I heard the magic words I had chased for a year: 'Veronica, you are an Ironman.'

# Chapter Nine
## *Love and Sunrise*

I first saw Dave at the swim squad at the Hong Kong University facilities on a Thursday evening in October 2011. Our coach, former Hong Kong Olympian Fenella, placed the swimmers on different lanes depending on their level. I was on lane 2, and lane 4 was the fastest. I left the changing room, and as I was touching the cool water with my toe before jumping into the pool, I saw a guy in lane 4 who looked like a Greek God emerging from a Giorgio Armani advertisement. He was tall with broad shoulders, and I noticed his dimples as he smiled at me. With dark hair and a pronounced jawline, he reminded me of Superman. I blushed as I smiled back and quickly jumped in the water, slightly relieved to hide in my lane. He had an Australian accent, and I heard his name was Dave. I wished I was wearing something other than a red swim cap, goggles, and an unsexy Speedo swimsuit, but it was too late, and he could not unsee me. When the session finished, he waved goodbye, and butterflies started swimming in my stomach.

Over the next few weeks, we saw each other at training, races, BBQs, and on Saturday nights, when we all went partying around Wyndham Street. Every time there was a group gathering, we ended up sitting together and chatting. He was originally from the Gold Coast in Australia and had moved to Hong Kong to work as a pilot for Cathay Pacific Airlines. We talked about sports, traveling, and life in Hong Kong. One evening, I was out with my friend Alia, who was visiting me from Abu Dhabi, and we bumped into Dave and his friend Pete on Hollywood Road as we were going for dinner.

I stopped to say, 'Hi,' and introduced my friend Alia, then we kept walking.

'Who was that? There's so much sparkle between you two,' Alia said with a cheeky tone. 'It's so obvious you like each other.'

I nodded with a pleased smile, enjoying the electrifying chemistry still in the air.

One Saturday night, on Halloween in 2012, I was having a drink with my girlfriends at the famous SOLAS club. I had arrived from a glamorous 30th birthday party at the Ritz-Carlton Hotel, where our faces were painted with dazzling makeup. I was wearing a metallic dark green strapless dress, and my long hair was pulled up. I was chatting with my friends, and suddenly, I noticed Dave was on the other side of the club with some of his pilot friends. When he saw me, he approached me and greeted me with two kisses.

'You look gorgeous,' he said. We started talking and dancing, and I forgot about everything else.

'Let me offer you a drink,' he suggested as he saw my empty glass.

He took my hand and led the way through the busy crowd. While we waited for the drinks, we looked at each other without saying a word. This time, there were no pool lanes for me to hide in, and luckily I wasn't wearing the swim cap and goggles. Someone dancing accidentally pushed me toward Dave, and I ended up in his arms. It was the perfect moment, the perfect time, and the perfect kiss. We spent the rest of the evening together, dancing and laughing. We kissed goodbye before I took a taxi home, and before going to bed, I received a message, 'Sweet dreams, Beautiful. I can't wait to see you again.'

Dave was leaving for New York the following day, but as soon as he returned, we went on our first official date. It was a brunch at my favorite restaurant, Oola. The brunch turned into a motorbike ride to the south of the Island, where we walked along the beach holding hands while watching the sunset.

'I think he's the one,' I told Vicky on the phone a few weeks later after I sent her a picture of us. 'Everything feels right when we are together. We both love cycling, going for long runs, and traveling the world. Plus, I love Australians,' I added jokingly.

'It sounds exhausting,' Vicky replied, laughing. 'He seems perfect for you. I have a good feeling, and by the way, he looks like Superman.'

Dave wasn't just a handsome guy who had come out of the triathlon Olympus. He had a magnetic personality that drew people to him. He was always upbeat and relaxed and cheered people at the end of the runs and the bike rides as he was always amongst the fastest. I loved how humble and unassuming he was. I loved his smile. I loved how he made me feel.

We continued to go on dates, and whenever he was in town, I would stay at his place in the neighborhood of Sheung Wan. One evening in February 2013, we were having Thai food at his home, and I sensed something was off. He was quiet and distant. He had been short in his messages the previous weeks, and we hadn't seen each other for a few days because he said he was tired from flying and the jetlag. I hadn't put any pressure and convinced myself we were taking things slowly.

'Is everything OK?' I asked. He paused, and his expression became serious and tense. He crossed his arms and said,

'There's something I need to tell you. I'm going through a

divorce, and it's taking a toll on me. Things are turning ugly with my ex, I'm surrounded by lawyers and legal bills, and I'm not in a good head space. I really like you, I like hanging out, but I'm not ready to commit to anything serious at the moment. I need some space.'

I felt like I had a knife going down my throat, but I did my best to mimic a smile and stay composed. I knew he was going through a divorce, but I didn't know any details. I remembered the previous weeks and how he had been more distant and evasive. He had barely called or texted but I had justified his absence with excuses. How could I have been so stupid? There were so many signs, but I had decided not to see them.

'I get it,' I said calmly. 'I don't want to pressure you, and I know you are going through a lot. I'm happy to take things slowly. I also want you to be in a good space, and you need to sort out your past before you can move on.'

I lied as best as I could. I stayed at his place until we finished dinner but decided to return home afterward. My bed felt cold and empty, and I woke up feeling lonely. We continued seeing each other for the next few weeks, but I sensed a wall around him that was becoming thicker. Our time together was always fun and special, but he would disappear for days, and I was left guessing. I missed him, his dimples, I missed waking up next to him, and I wanted to be the person he would text when he landed in his pilot uniform, but he wasn't ready.

In July 2013, he sent a message inviting me to drink on a rooftop in Sheung Wan. It was a Thursday evening, and I wore a little black dress I had just purchased. I was excited to see him for the first time in two weeks. When I arrived, he was already sitting on a high chair on the terrace. He was wearing a black collar shirt and dark blue jeans. He looked tired and had pronounced bags around his eye. I could tell he had not been sleeping much. As

## THE FLIGHT HOME

soon as I greeted him, I sensed the atmosphere was tense. We tried to chitchat, but he seemed uncomfortable.

'I wanted to have a conversation,' he said. 'I'm still going through a big mess; my head is all over the place.' He paused and sighed. 'I'm carrying too much luggage and don't want to drag you along. It's not fair to you. You are an incredible woman, and you deserve 100 percent, but I can't give it to you.'

I looked at him in the eye, nodding. The waiter arrived with the drinks. I sipped my sauvignon blanc, bit my bottom lip, and replied firmly, 'You are right. I don't want anything less than 100 percent. I wish you could give it to me, but you can't, so it's best if we leave things here and stop seeing each other.'

We tried to continue the conversation and talk about random things, but we were both uneasy. We had said all the words that needed to be said. I looked down and back at him and uttered, 'I think it's better if I go.'

He nodded and smiled, although it was a different type of smile. It was a goodbye. I looked down, and the silence was bitter.

'Take care,' I said as I turned around and walked toward the lift. I pressed the button and waited for what felt like an eternity. The lift door opened slowly, and I saw a young woman with a sad look and a broken heart. It was my reflection in the mirror. I pressed the button to the ground floor and decided to walk home. I was in no rush to go to an empty bed that would remind me this was the last page of our love story.

I pulled out my iPhone from my beige leather purse, scrolled through our pictures, and read our old messages. We seemed so happy. Was it all a lie? Was it just bad timing? I took a deep breath, hesitated, and deleted everything that reminded me of Dave, including his number. What I was trying to delete was the bitterness in my heart, but there wasn't a button for that, so I deleted everything else instead.

I didn't hear from Dave, and I tried to avoid him during the following weeks. I felt silly for not seeing the obvious earlier, and when my friends asked me about him, I replied vaguely, saying we were just friends and changed topics quickly to avoid giving any details and confronting the truth.

In August 2013, I flew to the Canary Islands to spend the summer with my family. On the first night, Mom had prepared a welcome dinner in her new place in Tenerife, where she was now living. It was a delicious seafood paella. Mom and Vicky were both excited and asked me about the Australian boy.

'There's no more Australian boy,' I replied assertively. 'I don't want to talk about it.'

They looked at each other discreetly, and as always, Vicky found some random story to distract us. Becoming a teacher made her a master of storytelling, and she always had fun anecdotes from the students in her school. We laughed like in the good old times, and no one mentioned the Australian boy again. On my way back, I was at Frankfurt Airport waiting for my connecting flight to Hong Kong. I entered a Starbucks and read the message on the blackboard while waiting for my Caramel Latte, 'If you love somebody, let them go, for if they return, they were always yours. If they don't, they never were.'

I read it again, and those words soothed my heart. For the first time, I didn't feel upset thinking about Dave. I was at peace with myself and with letting him go, and I was ready to find love that wasn't surrounded by walls.

In Hong Kong, I focused on training for the triathlon and my career at Apple. Between work and exercise, the weeks seemed to fly by. I had several races before the end of the year, and training always kept my mind busy.

'Have you thought of online dating?' Bea asked me one day

## THE FLIGHT HOME

as we were running on Bowen Road.

'I can't be bothered,' I replied with frustration. 'This whole online dating thing is not for me, and I don't have time to waste on dates unless he wants to train with me.'

October arrived, and I was excited about all the trips and competitions. I was participating in the Half-Ironman in Taiwan and doing a triathlon in Phuket in November. I was busy preparing, booking accommodation, and pushing my training. At work, I had a bigger team, and more Apple Stores were opening across Hong Kong and Asia. The weekends were filled with parties and social events. I started to go on dates, even if it was only a casual coffee or a drink after training, and it felt good to be liked and appreciated.

One Sunday afternoon in October 2013, I went to The Globe, a bar on Peel Street where the Tritons had organized a gathering to watch the *Tour de France*. Sunday afternoons were always relaxed as everyone had done the training for the week, and we could enjoy some time off the bike, the pool, and the running track and socialize without wearing our Lycra suits.

Hong Kong was still hot and humid, and I was wearing a pink summer dress with brown leather sandals. I was tanned from the training outside and toned.

'You are looking fit and race-ready,' my friend Billy said as I approached the large wooden table where everyone sat.

I blinked an eye, and as I looked around, I saw Dave in the corner of the table, staring at me. I felt my heart race. He had a big grin and said, 'Hi.' I discreetly smiled back, hiding my surprise as I didn't expect him to be there. I quickly looked away and joined the girls on the other side of the table. We were all in a good mood, and the vibe was festive. People were making jokes and ordering rounds of drinks. After greeting everyone, I stood up to go to the bar. While waiting for the server, I felt a presence next to me.

I heard, 'One beer and a glass of prosecco for the lady, please.' I recognized Dave's voice.

'How have you been?' he asked. He seemed a bit nervous, and as the drinks arrived, he handed me the glass.

'Cheers,' I replied, lifting my glass, 'I'm great. I had an amazing summer in Spain, and I'm excited about all the races coming up.'

I wasn't nervous or sad anymore. I was happy to see him after a few months, and he looked different; he seemed relaxed and at ease. He told me about his fishing trip in Australia and his promotion at work. We chatted, and I felt the chemistry again, just like on our first date, but I knew better and went back to the table with the group. I felt him looking at me, but I avoided eye contact. It was already 8:00 p.m., and the *Tour de France* had just finished. The next day, I had an early start and prepared to leave. Dave smiled as I waved goodbye to the group.

I walked home feeling confident. I was living life on my terms, and even if I was alone, I didn't feel lonely. Just before bed, I heard my phone beep with a message. Before I read it, I had the intuition that it was Dave. I recognized the number.

'It was nice to see you. You look great. Night, night.'

I woke up the following day and picked up my phone to reread the message. I smiled. Then I put the phone away and started thinking of the rooftop bar, the sour conversation, and the hundreds of shattered pieces of my heart I had picked up from the floor. I wasn't ready to have it broken again.

A week later, I received a second message from Dave inviting me to go on a hike before going to work. We used to hike up the Peak from Old Peak Road, chat, and run. I hesitated. I wrote a draft, deleted it, wrote a new message, and pressed send.

'Ok, let's meet at 6:30 a.m. at the escalator of Caine Road.'

## THE FLIGHT HOME

We met as the sun rose and chatted as we hiked up the steep hill. I was apprehensive and wanted to maintain the distance between us, but being together felt natural and effortless. We were both relaxed and open. We were like any other couple exercising together, except we were not a couple. Over the next few weeks, we started seeing each other more frequently; we rode up Mount Austin, went for hikes, started texting every day, and went for coffee and brunch dates on the weekend. He always suggested meeting up, and I was happy yet cautious to avoid crossing any line. We were just friends. When people asked me if I was dating anyone, I said, 'No.'

One day, we were having a coffee after going for a run. We were sitting at Oola, and his phone beeped with an email notification. He became serious as he picked up the phone and started reading the email. He was frowning, but suddenly his face changed, and he relaxed. He had a radiant smile and couldn't contain his excitement.

'It's done,' he said. 'The divorce, the lawyers, the fights, the fees. I finally can move on with my life without this massive burden.'

He was relieved, and the last brick of the wall surrounding him fell.

November arrived, and a big group of Tritons headed to Thailand to compete in the most anticipated event of the year: the Laguna Phuket Triathlon. It was a beautiful course that started with a swim in pristine waters, a bike ride along the tropical beaches and the local villages, and a run on the golf course. The best part was the party afterward, where everybody danced and celebrated the season's last race. I was staying at a villa I had rented with Bea, Jane, and a few other girls, and Dave was staying in a different one with the guys.

On race day, we all headed toward the transition area to

prepare our equipment. All the bikes had been checked in the previous day. I went to my spot, placed my running and bike shoes on the floor, hung my green visor from the bike handle, and pumped the tires. It was still dark, but a vibrant energy was in the air, with hundreds of people walking around excitedly, preparing for the big day. I looked at my gear one last time, mentally visualizing the race. The sunglasses, the energy gels, the race bib, everything was there, and I was ready. The sun was rising, and the loud music started playing on the speakers.

Then the race host announced, 'Good morning Phuket! Are you ... ready?'

Participants began whistling and clapping. My heart was racing fast. As I approached the wooden boat that transferred all participants to the start of the race on the beach, I bumped into Dave, who was wearing his deep blue triathlon suit. We hugged each other and jumped together on the boat. I was nervous, had butterflies, and couldn't wait for the race to start.

The gunshot announced the beginning of the swim, and all participants sprinted toward the water, trying to reach the front of the pack. Everyone ran against the waves, and I felt elbows, feet, and kicks. It was hectic and chaotic for a few minutes until the swimmers started to spread out in the water, and I finally found my rhythm. The bike ride was 55 km. and started with a tough steep hill. Many riders stepped off the bike and started walking. I managed to zig-zag up the mountain and ride the whole way up. Once I conquered the summit, I gained confidence and continued powering through the roads, speeding up on the flats and the downhills. The fun part started after passing along the beaches of Surin and Naithon. We rode through small villages where hundreds of Thai locals waited on the side of the road, clapping and with signs in Thai to cheer the participants. The villages were humble, and many children were barefoot but

## THE FLIGHT HOME

had lovely warm smiles and were having the time of their lives. As I rode by, a dozen of them were waving and screaming, 'Go, go, go,' in English, making me feel like a celebrity.

The run was 12 km. following a golf course track, and it was already 40°C Celsius by 10:00 a.m. The sun was intense, with no shade. I was tired but felt strong and had enough energy.

'Looking strong,' a man cheered as I passed him running.

I headed into the final 1 km., and I started hearing the music and the announcements from the microphone at the finish line. The adrenaline kicked in, and a sudden boost of energy took over. I started sprinting, passing people, and encouraging those who were shuffling. The finish line was so close now.

I was in the final stretch and could see the crowd around me cheering: my coaches Fenella and AM, my friend Jane, the other Tritons, and Dave. He was there, standing at the finish line, and as I crossed it, he hugged me. I was exhausted but wanted to savor the moment of conquering one more race.

I heard from the speakers, 'Congratulations, Veronica! 2nd in your age group.'

I stretched my arms in the air and smiled. 'A podium,' I yelled in disbelief.

Dave stared at me with proud eyes. We looked at each other and kissed. I didn't think about it. It felt right. Again, the perfect moment and the perfect kiss. He held my hands, and we walked away from the finish line.

'Would you give me a second chance?' he asked with a hesitant smile. I had a rollercoaster of emotions and felt on top of the world.

'It depends,' I replied with a grin. 'I only take 100 percent.'

'How about 200 percent? Do you think that's good enough?' he asked. I didn't reply, and we kissed again.

That evening we went together to the award ceremony. He

took a picture as I stepped on the podium to collect my award: a small elephant trophy with a golden plate that read Laguna Phuket Triathlon 2013.

We were both supposed to fly back to Hong Kong the next day, but we decided to extend our holiday to explore Phuket together. We rented a scooter and rode to the south, where we discovered a romantic resort on a hill with breathtaking ocean views. Holding hands, we watched the sunset from the cliff.

Back in Hong Kong, we started to spend more and more time together, and no walls were separating us this time. Three months later, in February 2014, he invited me to sail in Australia. I loved the idea of exploring his country with him, and sailing on a catamaran sounded like an adventure. We took off from Hervey Bay, on the Sunshine Coast, and sailed north to Fraser Island, the largest sand island in the world. It was sunny and warm, and we enjoyed watching the sunrise from the boat, spotting pods of dolphins and turtles, and counting the shooting stars from the deck at night. There were many.

Life with Dave turned into a constant adventure. We became a team and visited the world, from the exotic beaches of Boracay in the Philippines to the street markets in Hanoi, the nightlife of Tokyo, the waterfalls in Bali, the mountains of Whistler, the wildlife in South Africa, the Spatial Museum in New York and more.

In May 2014, we decided to move in together, and we rented a cozy rooftop apartment in the neighborhood of Sai Ying Pun. I had the life I had always dreamed of, and it felt like I had it all. In summer, I invited Dave to Spain for the first time, and Vicky and Mom giggled when I announced it.

'So, are we allowed to talk about the Australian boy then?' Vicky teased me on the phone.

As Christmas approached, we decided to spend a week in Bali

## THE FLIGHT HOME

in a boutique hotel in Canggu called United Colors of Bali, run by a French couple. It was secluded and romantic, with independent cabanas built in wood and bamboo, each with a different color theme. We spent five days in Villa Blue, enjoying the nature of Bali, running along the rice fields, visiting the Buddhist temples, eating Indonesian food, and surfing on the beach. In the evening, we enjoyed a glass of wine on our veranda, overlooking the rice paddies and talked about the future and all the places we wanted to visit.

We welcomed 2015 in Tugu Bali, a hotel inspired by Balinese culture and tradition, with dozens of art pieces, from chandeliers to Balinese masks, displayed in the lobby and along the halls. We entered through an outdoor corridor elegantly decorated with long bamboo poles on the sides. Soft Balinese music played in the background, and the lights were dimmed. The host led us to our dining table next to the stage, and a waiter welcomed us with a refreshing kalamansi cocktail and two colorful flower necklaces. Gracious Balinese ladies in traditional outfits and dramatic black makeup performed a traditional dance on stage, delicately moving their long fingers and nails to the sound of musical instruments. The dinner combined Western and Asian dishes with exotic flavors and ingredients like coconut, lime, and lotus leaves. When midnight arrived, all the guests were invited to the garden to watch the fireworks and celebrate the New Year.

'Happy New Year,' I whispered to Dave as he held me by the waist.

'Happy New Year, Beautiful,' he replied. 'To you, to us, and our life together. I love you.'

We kissed as the colorful fireworks brightened the sky. The DJ started playing music, and we went inside to dance. It was our first New Year's Eve together, and 2015 promised to be the best year ever.

Exactly one month later, in February, the best news took us by surprise. I exited the bathroom at home, feeling nervous and excited.

'Honey ... I'm pregnant,' I said with tears of joy as Dave sat on the couch. He rushed toward me, hugged me, and rubbed my tummy.

'Pregnant,' he repeated in shock, 'Wow, we are going to have a baby. You are going to be a wonderful mom.' In Bali, we had talked about our future, and we were both ready to start our little family together and decided to try for a baby. Thirty days later, it happened, and I felt like the lucky girl in the movie. I rubbed my belly and said with a grin, 'I have a feeling it's a girl. I want two girls, just like Vicky and me.'

My first pregnancy weeks were exciting and daunting, as everything was new. I downloaded an app that explained what happened week after week, and I kept informing Dave about the changes. 'This week, the baby is a bean,' 'now it's a blueberry.' Every night I read the book *What to Expect* in bed, occasionally caressing my belly and the little life growing inside. The pregnancy was barely noticeable, and I took pictures of my tummy in front of the mirror every day, trying to spot the first changes in my body. We were happy to keep our little growing secret, although we couldn't wait to tell the world. In only two more weeks, we would reveal the news to the world. I was counting the days on my calendar.

On week ten, after listening to the little racing heartbeat during the doctor's visit, we decided it was time to announce the pregnancy to my family in Spain. So, we organized a Skype video call with Mom, Vicky, my grandma, my uncles, aunts, and cousins. After a casual, nervous chitchat, I broke the news live. I was expecting the first grandchild in the family. Mom shed a tear, Vicky started crying, my grandma thanked God, and we

## THE FLIGHT HOME

all shared that special moment from opposite sides of the world.

Two weeks later, I was due for the three-month scan and was thrilled to say, 'Hello,' again to the little bean on the screen. I checked my app, and the baby was now the size of a plum. Dave was flying to Anchorage, Alaska, so I went to the clinic in Central alone during my lunch break. As Doctor Stevenson initiated the scan, I pulled out my iPhone.

'Please wait a moment,' I asked. 'I would like to take a video for my partner; he's flying at the moment, and I want to make sure he doesn't miss it.'

The doctor calmly prepared the equipment, and after a few seconds, we saw the tiny black shape on the screen, like in previous ultrasounds. There it was, our beautiful baby. I anxiously anticipated the loud and fast heartbeat as I recorded the scene. It was the sound of motherhood. But there was silence. We couldn't hear a sound. It was like a movie after pressing the pause button; no sound, no movement, no nothing, just a still image on a screen. I was still filming, trying to make sense of everything and attempting to press the play button of the little plum inside me. The doctor remained quiet, and the nurse, Michelle, gave me a compassionate look. He stopped the ultrasound, and suddenly, I knew. The world around me stopped moving, just like the little heart had stopped beating. Paralyzed, I looked at the dark screen in disbelief, holding my tears, trying to make the tiny seed move, shake, or do something. Anything.

'I'm sorry. There's no heartbeat,' the doctor announced, handing me a tissue.

On April 10$^{th}$, 2015, in that bright and sterile doctor's room, I went from being the lucky girl in the movie to becoming the character no one ever wants to play. My dreams were shattered in a few seconds, and I was mourning a little plum that was no longer beeping. I went home, looked for the picture of the previous ultrasounds I had kept in my jewelry box, and lay in bed, holding the image of the baby I would never meet. I cried and cried. I wanted to go back into the past. I wanted to go back to being a mom. Instead, I was saying goodbye alone to my baby with the only picture I would ever have.

I fell asleep for an hour and woke up confused and with a headache. I called Dave, who had just landed in the US, and he picked up the phone excitedly, expecting to watch the video. I thought I had been able to compose myself, but feeling his happiness made everything real again. I tried to explain what had happened, but after I uttered the first few words, I started sobbing uncontrollably. I hung up the phone and sent him a message explaining what had happened.

He replied, 'I love you. Always.'

The following weeks and months were slow and excruciating. All my close girlfriends started to announce pregnancies, and my Facebook feed became inundated with pictures of ultrasounds and baby showers. Some girls wore pink, others blue but my heart wore black. I saw babies and moms-to-be everywhere and hated myself and my flat belly. When my birthday arrived in June 2015, I turned thirty-five. In the morning, before going to work, I deleted Facebook account and felt relieved. My dream had been stolen, and I wanted to be alone. I only told my closest friends as most people didn't know about the pregnancy. When I shared the news, some replied, 'You will get pregnant again soon,' others thought they were comforting me, saying, 'Don't worry, miscarriages are very frequent,' and the majority shared a random story about their cousin or a neighbor who had also suffered a loss.

'No one understands,' I told Dave in the evening as he tried to cheer me up. 'No one realizes I was the mom of that baby. Another one won't replace the pain.' Dave looked at me in

## THE FLIGHT HOME

silence. He knew no words would make me feel better, so he took me in his arms and held me tight against him as tears rolled down my cheek.

Five months later, in November 2015, I was pregnant again, although we were more cautious this time, and I decided not to talk about it. I deleted the pregnancy app, avoided reading about motherhood, and let things flow. I kept myself busy to prevent myself from thinking about babies. In January 2016, as I was starting to believe I would finally be a mom, I suffered another miscarriage. It was the week after I was promoted at Apple, and all my colleagues congratulated me in the corridor and the stores, making my loss even more painful and invisible. I said goodbye to another baby I would never meet.

'I'm sorry, little one,' I whispered in Spanish, rubbing my tummy as the doctor explained the procedure while I was lying in the hospital bed. 'I wish I could protect you.'

Dave was holding my hand. The nurse injected me with general anesthesia, and everything became blurry until I lost consciousness. I went home that night feeling empty. There was nothing in my tummy, nothing in my heart. It was shattered once again. Would I be able to pick up the pieces one more time?

A year and a half after losing our babies, I had given up hope of carrying a pregnancy to term. I did not belong to the group of pregnant girls, and no one saw me as a mom, even if I had carried my babies for almost three months. Like many others suffering in silence, I was an invisible mom and couldn't find my place.

One evening in April 2016, I came home after work. We had just purchased our first flat together. It was a small but lovely apartment in Kennedy Town with a big terrace. It was already dark when I opened the door.

'Surprise,' said Dave with a big grin while filming. It wasn't my birthday, and we were not celebrating anything special, so I was confused. I saw a dark blue cushion on the other side of the living room with something moving inside. Curious, I moved closer and discovered a small puppy. It was a French Bulldog with brindle fur, and when I tried to touch it, it reached out to my fingers with its playful paws and started licking my hand. It was tiny and had disproportionately big ears, making it look cute and funny.

I gently picked up the puppy. 'He's adorable. What's his name?' I asked Dave, who was still filming.

'His name is Django,' he replied as I patted his soft fur. And that's how Django came into my life. Although he chewed every piece of furniture, he proved there was still room for love in my heart.

Two back-to-back pregnancies resulting in silent miscarriages had scarred me for life, and we had decided to start looking at alternative options. I had researched the tedious, painful, and expensive process of IVF and decided to initiate the treatment. It was very different from how I had dreamed of having a baby, but my hopes of becoming a mom slowly faded.

The clinic shared all the information about the treatment, side effects, and price with us. A few days later, I went for my first check-up before starting the journey. The doctor scheduled a routine scan to ensure everything was in order. Dave joined me, and we watched silently as the nurse prepared the equipment. The doctor began to perform the ultrasound. I was counting how many times I had gone through the same routine. Too many. I looked at the doctor and noticed he was frowning, and his facial expression changed. I panicked, fearing there was something wrong.

'Well, well,' he said, visibly surprised. 'It seems you might not need any treatment after all. Your baby is already here.'

I stared at Dave in shock; he looked as confused as I was. I

## THE FLIGHT HOME

had a hundred questions but was unable to articulate any.

'A baby?' I repeated, puzzled, as I looked at a little dark shade on the monitor.

'Congratulations are in order,' Doctor Stevenson said with a warm and composed smile, removing his glasses. It seems we are going to be discussing something else today. Let me check the due date.' He put the scan measurements into the computer and announced, '26th of January 2017,' he winked at Dave. 'Make sure you are not flying.'

'Australia day,' Dave added with excitement, and we both started laughing, still in awe at the extraordinary news. I embraced the unexpected news with joy and hope, but I went to bed every night, wondering whether the little one was still moving inside me or the movie was on pause again. Every time I went to the bathroom, I became nervous at the thought of finding blood afterward. I tried not to obsess over the pregnancy and disconnected until we were well beyond the first trimester. I asked Dave not to buy anything related to babies or pregnancy. I didn't want to choose between blue and pink. I was too scared it would end up in black.

In July, at the three-month mark, we were in Italy for a friend's wedding, and on a sunny morning, we were having breakfast on the terrace of our hotel in Venice when I received a call from Hong Kong. I recognized the clinic's number and answered as nervous as I had ever been. It was Nurse Michelle. She had been with me from the beginning, from the first pregnancy, holding my hand when Dave wasn't there and handing me tissues to dry my tears. My hands were shaking, and my mouth was dry.

'Veronica, David, we have great news,' she said with a positive tone. 'The baby is fine. All the genetic results came back, and everything is normal. Do you want to know the gender?'

I had the phone on speaker. 'Yes, please,' I replied anxiously, holding Dave's hand from across the table.

'Congratulations, it's a girl,' she announced in excitement.

I thanked Michelle, hung up the phone, and started repeating with tearful eyes,'It's a girl; it's a girl. We are team pink.'

Dave smiled. I couldn't contain my emotions, so the Italian waiters overheard our conversation.

'*Brava, brava, una bambina,*' they congratulated me in Italian.

After breakfast, we walked along the canals of Venice and took pictures in front of the gondolas. I stopped at a street stand selling children's clothes. I grabbed a dress with pink and white stripes, felt the soft fabric, and imagined my baby girl wearing it. Seconds later, I put it back. What if I lost my baby again? What if the dress became a painful reminder of a baby I didn't have the chance to hold? I wasn't ready to become a mom and lose it all again. Without me noticing, Dave was watching from behind. He picked the same dress from the hanger, handed it to the Italian lady, and firmly told her we were buying it while rubbing my unnoticeable pregnant belly.

'Your baby?' the lady asked in English with a thick Italian accent. I hesitated, thinking of my answer. Dave handed her a twenty Euro note and replied, placing his hand on my tummy.

'Yes, our baby. We are expecting a girl.' It was Alba's first dress.

Shortly after the Italy trip, we had the summer holidays coming up, and we went back to Fraser Island to sail again. It had been our first holiday as a couple, and it was the perfect time to go back, two years later, this time with a very special guest on board. The weather was beautiful, sunny but chilly in the mornings and evenings, as it was winter in Australia. We spent the days on the boat, sailing with the wind, enjoying the sunshine, reading books, and occasionally going to the beach to walk on the sand and explore the island. I started showing a little belly and was feeling more tired than usual but glowing with happiness. I had begun reading about motherhood again without feeling anxious, and Dave was over the moon to become a dad and build our little family together.

On our last day, we planned to picnic on the beach in the afternoon and watch the sunset from the island. We packed a basket with some cheese and cold cuts with some beers for him and juice for me. As we reached the beach, he convinced me to climb a big dune. I looked up, took a deep breath, and jokingly protested.

'It looks like Everest to me.'

Dave took my hand and started pulling me along. 'Come on, you will love the views, and we don't want to miss the sunset.' After a long and slow hike on the sand, we reached the top of the dune, and Dave was right. The views were breathtaking, with an infinite ocean that changed colors from green to blue.

'Look, over there,' Dave said, pointing toward our catamaran. A pod of playful dolphins was swimming, jumping up and down. I pulled a blue sarong from my backpack, spread it on the sand, and prepared the picnic. As I turned around, Dave was on one knee, looking at me with a big smile.

'Veronica, will you marry me?' He was holding a white gold diamond ring in his right hand. I had never seen Dave nervous before. Surprised, I covered my mouth with my hands.

I looked at the beautiful ring and replied, 'Yes, a million times yes.'

He slid the ring on my finger, and I was mesmerized by the stunning glow of the diamond and the sparkle in Dave's eyes. I wanted that magical moment to last forever. The sun was setting on the horizon, the sand felt soft and warm on my feet, and my heart was filled with love.

I said, 'Yes,' a dozen more times in all six languages, kissing the father of my baby on top of Everest.

In the early hours of the 26th of January 2017, Dave and I took a taxi to Queen Mary Hospital, near our home in Kennedy Town. It was exactly forty weeks of pregnancy, and the doctors had decided to induce me because the baby was measuring small in the scans. I went in slightly nervous but confident, having taken a prenatal course with the midwives the months before. After years of waiting, I was ready to become a mom and finally hold my baby in my arms. I checked in to the pre-labor ward, changed my clothes into loose, light pink pajamas, and the nurse took me to a separate room where Dave was already waiting.

The nurse initiated the induction by injecting me with some drugs. As the chemicals started to kick into my body, the contractions escalated from zero to a million in minutes. I had never experienced such an intense pain. I tried to breathe and stay calm, but I couldn't and started screaming. I asked for the epidural to attenuate my excruciating contractions, but the only anesthetist on duty was busy with other emergency patients. Two hours later, sweating between contractions, I begged to try again, but the timing couldn't be worse.

The nurse explained, 'It's Chinese New Year, and all the other anesthetists are off duty celebrating the holiday. Try to take deep breaths; she will come as soon as she's available.'

Labor was becoming long and complicated. There was no progress after ten hours, and the pain worsened as I lost energy. I was dehydrated but was not allowed to drink any fluids. The nurse only gave me one small ice cube every twenty minutes, which melted in my mouth after a few seconds. Then, the painful countdown of the twenty minutes reset.

The anesthetist never came despite my animal screams begging for help. After twelve hours of induction and contractions, the doctors announced they would proceed with

## THE FLIGHT HOME

an emergency C-section for the baby's sake. I was nauseous and sweaty and had no strength left to protest. I stared at the monitor to ensure the baby's heart was beeping. Dave held my hand and removed the sweat from my forehead with a wet towel.

Two nurses asked me to sit in a wheelchair, and they wheeled me to the operating theatre. The air was frigid, and two doctors were waiting for me, preparing tools, checking monitors, and speaking very fast in Cantonese. The same nurses helped me stand up and lie on the bed, and they tied my hands to the bedside rails.

I looked at Dave, confused and panicked. 'I'm scared,' I uttered quietly, 'What if something goes wrong?'

Dave comforted me with his calm voice.

'Queen Mary is known as the best hospital for natal care in Hong Kong and has world-class facilities to look after newborns,' he said.

I knew all that, but I was terrified and never expected to go for an emergency C-section. No one told me what was wrong.

I was too exhausted and dizzy to process the chaos around me. The anesthetist injected the drugs through a long needle. I clenched my fists and closed my eyes as the needle broke through the skin on my back. There were noises, bright lights, and fast conversations in Cantonese. I was cold and sweaty at the same time. A nurse asked me if I could feel my feet and my legs. I moved my toes, then moved them again, and a few minutes later, I was completely numb in my lower body. She announced the procedure was about to begin.

The nurses had placed a long black curtain on my upper stomach to prevent me from watching the surgery. I was too weak and scared to ask any questions and just wanted the torture to end and hold my baby in my arms. I looked at the clock. It was 10:45 p.m. Restrained, I squeezed Dave's hands with strength and waited. I kept on staring at the clock. It was now 10:51 p.m.

I heard noises, but I couldn't feel anything. After a distinctive suction noise, the doctor announced in English, 'Time of birth, 10:57 p.m.'

Then I heard the first scream of our baby. Alba. I could hear her; I could feel her. Our little rainbow baby was finally here. Her scream filled the room with life and my heart with love. The nurses carried her quickly to one side of the room for a standard check-up and a clean-up. I thought they were preparing her for handover to me for the precious skin-to-skin moment my midwives had prepared me for.

I waited a few minutes, but the nurses didn't bring her to me. I stretched my arms in the air, signaling that I was ready to hold my baby. Instead, they rushed out of the room, taking little Alba away, wrapped in a dark blue blanket with the initials QM for Queen Mary. They didn't let me see her before leaving the room and shutting the door.

Confused, I remained in bed, looking at Dave inquisitively, trying to understand what had just happened. The surgeon was concentrated on sewing my stomach, and Dave was looking around, trying to make eye contact with someone who could give us an explanation. He was trying to remain calm, but I could sense his anxiety.

A nurse in a light green uniform entered the room and addressed us. 'Your baby needs assistance to breathe. They are taking her to the ICU on the sixth floor.'

'She can't breathe?' I asked in shock. 'ICU? Will she be OK?'

The nurse explained that Alba would be admitted to the intensive care unit and that the pediatrician would give us more details in the morning. She asked me to sign a consent form, and before I could enquire any further, babbling in Cantonese she left the operating theatre in crisis mode to rush after the other nurses.

## THE FLIGHT HOME

Minutes later, the same nurse asked Dave to follow her, and he left after kissing me on the cheek. Once my stitches were completed, a nurse I didn't recognize came and wheeled my bed to a waiting room next door, where I was left alone, with no one to talk to, no phone, no Alba. A big round-shaped clock on the wall was ticking as a million thoughts spun through my head. All I wanted to know was whether Alba was alive and healthy, but there was no answer in that cold empty room.

Fifteen minutes later, which felt like an hour, the nurse returned. She helped me sit in a wheelchair and took me to the maternity ward, where all the new mothers, mostly local Chinese, and their new-born babies were recovering after labor, separated by thin curtains between their beds. The nurse knew nothing about Alba except that she was taken to the ICU. It was already 1:30 a.m., but the ward was noisy with babies crying. I inspected the large room, and based on the number of rows, there were close to eighty mommies. I noticed a few new moms awkwardly wandering around. Many were walking slowly to and from the bathroom, with their hands on their back in visible pain. I was given a name tag with the number 33, and the nurse pointed toward one empty bed in the middle of the room while calling me "Mommy 33".

Many Hong Kong parents had strategically planned the conception of their baby to schedule the delivery during Lunar New Year, which is a good omen. So the room was crowded with lucky moms and their Lunar New Year babies. But Mommy 33 didn't have a baby with her; as visitors were not allowed during the night, I spent that first night alone, wondering if my baby would live to see the sunrise in the morning.

Sometime between my scary thoughts and failed attempts at sleeping, the sun rose the following morning. At 8:00 a.m., when the room opened to allow visitors, Dave found me in bed number 33. I was still not able to walk, but I started to feel my legs and could move my toes. With his help, I managed to sit in the wheelchair. We went to the corridor and waited for the lift to go up to the ICU floor to talk with the doctors and meet little Alba, who had spent her first night alone in an incubator.

The pediatrician was a petite Indian woman with a soft voice and a British accent who explained that the baby had suffered stress during labor, and could still not breathe independently. Therefore they had to intubate her to assist her with breathing and feeding.

'Will she be OK?' I asked nervously, looking up at her from the wheelchair.

The doctor replied in a firm but compassionate tone, 'It's too early to say, but be assured your baby is in the best hands, and we are looking after her day and night to give her the best chance.'

'Thank you,' I replied.

She looked at the file she was carrying one more time and said, 'Alba, what a beautiful name. What does it mean?'

'Alba means sunrise in Spanish.' We both smiled, and she excused herself as the nurse called her from behind.

A male nurse led us to the intensive care unit. As the door opened, I saw a large room with a dozen incubators, some empty, some with tiny babies inside. I looked around, and some were smaller than a little mouse. Each was a little fighter, busy fighting for their own life inside a cold plastic container, away from their parents. I felt a shiver run through me.

Dave continued to wheel me slowly, and finally stopped. I read the tag in the incubator. It was Alba. I was meeting my daughter for the first time. I looked at her, and she looked at me. She had big expressive blue eyes with a hint of green. She seemed alert and was trying to move around, staring at me. She had three tubes running from her nose and mouth and another

## THE FLIGHT HOME

attached to her arm through her little vein to feed her. I tried to hold my tears. I was ecstatic to be a mom, but the thick plastic wall of the incubator separating us was a cruel reminder that I could lose her at any time. I knew Dave was thinking the same thing, and without saying a word, we held hands.

'She's beautiful,' he said while I nodded.

Something magical happened as I looked at her a second time. Although the doctor had warned us about her fragile condition, I saw life in her eyes and strength in her little kicks.

Without overthinking it, I confidently said, 'She's a fighter. Somehow I know in my heart she's going to be OK.' In the same way that, fifteen years earlier, I knew in my heart that Dad would go, now I was certain that Alba would live.

Dave and I left the hospital that evening with our empty baby car seat, a pink bag full of girl onesies, some nappies, and jumped in a taxi without our baby. I had been discharged, but Alba hadn't. The following days were intense and hard, and mixed emotions blurred them, as we were only allowed to visit Alba during limited hours, three times a day. I took every opportunity to be there, talk to her, feed her with a bottle, and finally hold her in my arms for a few minutes when they removed the last tube. The first time I was allowed to breastfeed her, I cried in the nursery room beside the incubators. She was sucking my breast, looking in all directions while moving her little legs and arms, trying to make sense of her new world, while I was looking at her, mesmerized by the amount of happiness she had already brought into my world.

'I'm going to take you to your real home with Mommy and Daddy.' I told her while I rocked her to sleep.

A week later, on February 3rd, she was out of the incubator, and we brought her back home, where she slept in her cot for the first time in her short life. In a matter of days, Alba turned our world upside down. I became used to little sleep, long days, and short nights interrupted by feeding and crying. Although my C-section recovery was painful, it was nothing compared to the fear of losing my baby, and having her in my arms made the physical pain irrelevant. I was on parental leave for four months, enjoying every little motherhood moment before returning to work.

As soon as I was given the green light to walk and exercise moderately, I started to hike up the Peak at sunrise with Alba in my little carrier and Django on the leash. Dave joined us when he was not working, running up to the top and waiting for us there. We loved our little family life and did everything together. We exercised, went out for brunch, I read books in Spanish to Alba, and as soon as she had her passport, we traveled around the world. We first flew from Hong Kong to Spain to visit my family in the Canary Islands. From there, we went to Washington to attend the wedding of my Brazilian friend Carla, and a few days later, we made our way back to Hong Kong, completing a full circle around the globe.

On September 23rd, 2017, we hosted our wedding celebration. We wanted a destination wedding so that friends from around the world could come and make a holiday out of it. We chose Ibiza, knowing the White Island would be an attractive destination for singles and families, and it would be convenient for my family to attend.

We didn't want a religious ceremony but a casual, untraditional, fun wedding, and we found a Swiss celebrant, Pierre, to help us conduct it in English and Spanish. My grandma Mari, being very traditional and religious, struggled to understand the concept of a non-religious wedding with a non-religious celebrant and made known her version of the facts, telling her friends and everyone back in the village that

## THE FLIGHT HOME

her granddaughter was being married by a hippy priest.

As I walked down the aisle with my beige lace gown and long veil Mom had helped me choose, I looked around and saw my entire life displayed in front of me, my childhood in France and Brazil, my challenges in Holland, my university friends, and my many years in Asia.

Vicky was my Maid of Honor, and my seven bridesmaids, who had come from all over the world, walked before me in light pink dresses holding arms with the elegant groomsmen who had traveled from Australia. The love of my life was at the end of the aisle of white petals, looking at me the way every girl wants to be looked at. I felt a soft breeze as I walked to the sound of the piano playing the melody, *One Thousand Years*. Only Dad was missing. I had asked his best friend, Jose, to walk me down the aisle on his behalf, and I'm sure Dad blinked an eye from his little spot in heaven with a glass of Campari and a Cuban cigar.

We had a romantic ceremony with Alba sitting on my lap, playing with her little fingers while the hippy priest talked about the elements of nature and the essence of love. Our mothers blessed our wedding rings, and we exchanged our vows overlooking the Mediterranean Sea.

When it was my turn, I looked at Dave, smiled, and started reading,

*'Dave, my love, my true love, You are my biggest adventure. Since our very first day together four years ago, I knew deep in my heart you were the one. Falling in love with you was easy. You showed me respect and care, love and inspiration, you became my partner in crime, my best friend, my lover, and my soul mate. And somehow, when two soul mates meet, the Universe blinks an eye. Today is the happiest day of my life. And I want to say thank you for being the amazing partner and father you are and the amazing husband I know you will be. You have given me more than I could ever ask for, and our beautiful little family,*

with Alba and our little puppy Django, are the most precious gift life could offer me. So today, it's also about saying thanks. Gracias.'

'I promise to love you on the sunny days and the rainy days. I will try hard to be a better version of myself day-by-day, to listen and to share, to trust you, to forgive you because we all make mistakes, and to never shut down on you. I promise to share your dreams and hopes, and I will try to help you when you need it, but also to give you your space when you don't.'

'I will try my best to be a role model for our little Alba, and I am sure together we will raise a kind and beautiful young woman – and I am also sure you will scare the boys away'.

'I promise never ever to give up on us and never to lose faith in us. What we have is very precious, and just like anything precious, we have to love it and cherish it to keep it alive.'

'Today, I want to promise, in front of our dear friends and family, that I will be faithful to you and to us and that I will take care of you throughout this magical journey as we grow old together. I give myself to you with all my heart, and I will love you today and every day for the rest of my life. You are my biggest adventure.'

With a cheeky smile, the celebrant announced, 'You may now kiss the bride,' and we had our first kiss as Mr. and Mrs. Smith.

The guests clapped and threw white petals as we walked back along the aisle, and the party started with champagne, cocktails, Spanish canapes, and happy faces everywhere. It was the wedding I had always dreamed of with the man I had fallen in love with, surrounded by family and friends, and enjoying life to the fullest with a baby in my arms. A local band played Flamenco Jazz while the sun set on the horizon, and a professional Spanish ham cutter quickly became more popular than the newlyweds.

For our first dance as husband and wife, Dave and I impersonated Olivia Newton-John and John Travolta, dancing to the lyrics *Summer Nights* from the musical, Grease. We had rehearsed the choreography at home and put our skills to practice on the dance floor. Shortly after, our bridesmaids and grooms joined us on stage, and the rest of the guests started dancing too. It was a magical day on a magical island.

We spent our honeymoon on the neighboring island, Formentera, which is much quieter and more laid-back than the glamorous Ibiza. Alba was with us, and it was even more special because we had our little rainbow to remind us how lucky we were to be a family.

With the craziness of the wedding preparation, the dress fitting, the rehearsals, and all the logistics behind it, Dave and I hadn't had a chance to discuss our future or any plans about growing our little family. After all the suffering and the loss I had gone through, I felt Alba was my miracle baby, my sunrise, and I didn't dare to ask life for more. My dream was to have two daughters close in age because of my special relationship with Vicky. She was my best friend, my Maid of Honor, and my biggest confidant. I wanted the same for Alba but wasn't prepared to endure the suffering again. We didn't plan anything; we didn't have any expectations. We were just a couple of newlyweds enjoying life with a baby ... Or two.

Exactly nine months after our wedding, one day before my birthday, our second daughter was born on the 24th of June 2018. We called her Maia, and I told the nurses she was a present from life for my birthday. Labor was smoother, and although I still had to go through an emergency C-section, I could hold her against my skin as soon as she entered the world. She was a beautiful, healthy baby with hazel eyes and olive skin. She was born smiling, and as soon as we were able to bring her home, Alba fell in love with her too. Django approached the new little stranger and suspiciously sniffed her little feet. A few seconds later, he started licking her toes while Alba giggled and repeated,

'Baby Maia.' They were seventeen months apart, the same age difference as Vicky and me.

A few months later, I discovered that Maia means love in Nepalese. Maia and Alba, love and sunrise.

# Chapter Ten
## Closing the Loop–Resilience

On the 6th of December 2021, the flight from Madrid to Sydney with a stopover in Dubai was as smooth as a thirty-hours-plus journey around the world with two little ones can be. Airplanes are always a novelty for kids, like a gigantic toy in real life, and Alba and Maia kept themselves busy pressing every single button, opening and closing the windows, and watching cartoons, while I apologized left, right, and center to the neighbors around us. I was reminded of my first long flight to Rio de Janeiro thirty years earlier and how important I felt flying around the world inside a gigantic Jumbo.

At Sydney airport, we went through immigration and on to our Airbnb flat in Allawa, twenty minutes outside of Sydney, where we quarantined for five days, as required by the state of New South Wales. Being locked inside a flat was painful and tedious, especially after the long trip, but as soon as we were free to leave, we rented a car and started to make our way north to the Gold Coast to visit Dave's family. We drove up the Pacific Highway singing *Hakuna Matata*, counting the cows and horses along the way, while I answered a million, 'Whys,' and, 'Are we there yets?' After a short break for two nights in stunning Suffolk Park on the outskirts of Byron Bay, we made it to the Gold Coast on the 23rd of December 2021, right on time for Christmas.

We had already spent several Christmas holidays in Australia with Dave's family in previous years, but this time it was special because the pandemic had kept us apart for two years. It had been five months since we had left Hong Kong on what was supposed to be a three-week holiday, and we were hopeful that the restrictions would be lifted and would finally be able to return home in January.

Alba and Maia loved spending time with their grandparents and cousins, spotting kangaroos in the fields, playing in Kurrawa Park, and not having to wear masks or shoes. It turns out Australians don't like to wear shoes much. This contrasted with Hong Kong, where masks were still mandatory; the girls embraced the Aussie lifestyle and breathed in the freedom.

We were staying off Broadbeach Waters on the Gold Coast in the family house by the canals, where the girls enjoyed daily walks along the sandy canal beach. They fed families of black swans and looked for curious stingrays that came to chill by the side of the pontoons. As I followed them, my feet were sandy, and my heart felt warm. My daughters were becoming true Aussies, and we were all enjoying the new life Down Under, without worrying about quarantining and being sent to Penny Bay.

Dave and I were hopeful that things might improve in Hong Kong as the rest of the world was moving on and starting to live with the virus rather than trying to eradicate it. Life was slowly returning to normal, and we were confident Hong Kong would be next. The good news never came. Instead, the Delta variant of COVID-19 took South Africa by surprise in early December 2021, and soon spread worldwide. Hong Kong immediately started banning passenger flights from the affected countries, and Australia was added to the blacklist in a matter of days. This new curveball meant that we were officially not allowed to

## THE FLIGHT HOME

return to our country, our puppy, our home, and our life. I had been waiting for five months, and now I had lost hope that the good news would ever arrive. I sighed in disbelief as I watched the news on TV.

Days later, I decided to close my new logistics business, as the major ports in China were paralyzed due to the constant outbreaks, and my company wasn't generating any revenue. My old life was falling apart before my eyes, and I was figuring out how to pick up the pieces from another continent. That evening I called Mom, who was waking up in the Canary Islands. I started talking and burst into tears.

'Mom,' I sobbed, 'everything we own and have built is in a place we cannot return to. We have worked so hard for years, and now I feel I'm losing everything.' My voice was shaky.

'You haven't lost anything,' Mom replied, 'You can find a job, build a new home, and start over. You have your health, and you are everything you need.'

She was right. Her words comforted me, and I thought of Dad and what losing everything really meant.

We spent the afternoon of December 31st in Burleigh Heads, sitting on the grass, eating fish and chips from the local shop. Dave and I watched Alba and Maia play in the park while we watched the surfers catch the last waves of the year. It was the same way we had spent New Year's Eve two years previously, right before the world pressed pause, by using the pandemic button. The orange sun was starting to set on the horizon, and a pleasant summer breeze blew my hair backward.

David lifted his plastic cup and said, 'This year was crazy, but we made it, and look at us. Here we are. Are you worried about what's next?'

He held my hand as I looked at the ocean and calmly replied, 'My dad always said I would always be OK no matter what. He taught me not to worry about things I can't control. I don't know what will happen, but somehow in my heart, I know we will be fine.'

'Your dad was a wise man,' said Dave, 'I wish I had had the chance to meet him.'

I lifted my glass toward Dave, and we both cheered, 'To us, our little family, and our unknown future.'

The sound of the waves was soothing. There is something magical about spending New Year's on a beach, by the sea. I thought of my childhood in Rio de Janeiro, where the tradition is for millions of people to dress up in white and head to the beach with a bottle of champagne and white flowers. The flowers are then thrown into the sea to honor the Goddess of the Ocean called Yemanja. I have always loved this ritual and have since associated New Year's Eve with the ocean. Besides the usual resolutions of getting fitter or reading more, this year we had to face the biggest decision of all—what were we going to do with our lives? Hong Kong had shut its doors indefinitely, but did we want to wait? Were we going to continue living in this nomadic limbo?

In the evening, I sent an email to the kindergarten in Hong Kong explaining that what had started as a temporary overseas stay had now become permanent, and we were withdrawing our daughters for good. The decision was made. We had rolled the dice of life. In the meantime, I also applied for a spouse visa to allow me to live and work in Australia and find a job as soon as possible. With my business closed and the global crisis, I now had no home to return to, no job, and no school for our girls. And soon, my husband would be gone also. Dave still had his job as a pilot at Cathay Pacific to go back to, our home, our dog, and he couldn't suddenly leave everything behind and re-settle in Australia.

## THE FLIGHT HOME

We said goodbye to 2021, with fireworks in the sky, and when we woke up the following day, on January 1, 2022, the girls and I officially started our new life in Australia while Dave was trying to find a way to go back to Hong Kong, to be separated once again indefinitely. We had accidentally moved to a new country with only one purple suitcase, leaving everything behind us.

Having moved many times before, I knew the drill well—plan to move, prepare the paperwork, and research areas to live and schools. Also, in the past, we had a job lined up already. Then movers make our furniture and belongings disappear into big carton boxes, and we say goodbye to our friends, host a farewell party, board our plane, and wave goodbye. That's how moving was done in the past, no matter where the destination was.

This time, we had moved to another country on another continent, and we were doing the same drill but starting from the end, like building a house from the roof. We were playing a movie starting from the last scene and going backward.

I spent the following weeks filing paperwork around the Gold Coast: enrolment for Broadbeach Kindergarten and State School, forms for job interviews, application forms for Medicare cards, and spouse visa documents. I had piles of documents on the dining table that kept on growing every day. It was non-stop and mentally draining. The spouse visa, in particular, was a nightmare. Although Dave and I had been married for over five years and had two children together, I had to provide witness testimonials, photographic evidence, original copies of our birth certificates, Facebook posts, and even a statutory declaration of our relationship history.

'I have the feeling the paperwork is never going to end,' I told Dave in frustration, pulling my hair back with both hands.

Dave was able to extend his stay in Australia until the end of January by using up his entire annual leave for the year and adding unpaid leave. We were fortunate to stay in his mother's house, especially considering the astronomical rental prices throughout the country. I felt lucky to have Dave's parents around, who treated me like a daughter and welcomed us with open arms.

The Gold Coast had attracted thousands of families from New South Wales, Victoria, and overseas who were tired and frustrated with the social restrictions and wanted a change in their lifestyle.

At the school preparation talk, the Principal jokingly said, 'The school happily welcomes children from all places, but we might put a quota on the Victorians.'

Out of 1,171 students at Broadbeach State School, four hundred families, over a third were international, so they did welcome everyone with open arms.

From the moment we decided that the girls and I would live in Australia, I started looking at the country and everything around us through a different lens. Unlike all the previous times I had visited, I was not a tourist anymore. The first months with Dave were a warm oasis. We organized little weekend getaways and went sailing with our daughters, who thought it was the most fun adventure ever. We did, too; watching them snorkel on Moreton Island, running on the beach, waking up in a catamaran in the middle of the ocean, and counting the stars at night were sweet memories I would keep in my iPhone and my heart. Life was messy and spontaneous, but it was good, and I was grateful. I knew Dave would have to leave us soon to return to Hong Kong, but I didn't want to think about that, and just enjoy the moment.

One day I asked the girls whether they preferred to live in Hong Kong, Spain, or Australia. Alba replied spontaneously, 'My favorite place is wherever we are all together as a family.'

## THE FLIGHT HOME

Those words broke my heart a little because she was speaking the truth.

At the same time, I began job hunting. I was planning to secure a job within a few months to resume my career, earn money, and climb the corporate ladder again. I curated ten types of CVs depending on the role and industry, customized cover letters, and spent hours browsing the web daily, screening jobs posted on LinkedIn and Seek. Friends in Australia had reassured me that the market was booming and I would find a job in a heartbeat. The weeks passed, and the "No thank yous" and "Keep an eye for future job openings" emails started to pile up in my inbox. The rejection folder was becoming thicker every day, and I was feeling demoralized and beginning to worry.

My international experience seemed irrelevant in the local market, my languages were no more than nice to have, and my biggest disadvantage was that I didn't have a network in Australia. Finding jobs is a people business; it's all about relationships, and that's when I heard for the first time the expression, your network is your net worth. I had none.

At the end of January, it was time to say goodbye to Dave without knowing when we would see him next. He would endure the hotel quarantine upon arrival, and we didn't know when or if the girls and I would be able to return to Hong Kong. Farewells are always difficult; this one was harder because it was an open-ended chapter with a blank page at the end.

Alba and Maia hugged Dave, climbing one leg each, saying, 'Don't go, Daddy. You always go. Why can't you live with us like the other daddies?'

I joined in as Maia said in her baby voice, 'Family huggy, family huggy.' We all started laughing, wrapped in bittersweet hugs.

My stomach tightened as I closed the door, waving goodbye

to Dave, who jumped in an Uber to go to Brisbane Airport. I was relieved Django, who was staying with our friends, would finally have his daddy, and this time Maia would not forget how to speak English. Not having a date for his return made the goodbye sour, especially after the long months we had spent separated in Spain. I didn't want to think about it; I had to focus and make it work for our family. I needed to find a good job so that we could afford to live in Australia and make the move permanent. For Dave, the pandemic had decimated the aviation industry, and finding a job in Australia as a pilot would be difficult and poorly paid. We didn't have a plan B, but we didn't have a plan A either.

The first day of school and kindergarten in February 2022, is when it hit me that this was now home for the three of us. I kissed Alba goodbye in her new pink and purple uniform as the bell of her new school rang, and she blended in with all the other children who were wearing identical black hats. It was the third school start the girls had had in less than a year, beginning in August 2021, in Hong Kong, September in Spain, and now January 2022, in Australia. Three different bells on three different continents, in four different languages: Mandarin, Cantonese, Spanish, and English. There was no doubt these little nomads were my daughters, and for them, all school bells sounded the same.

I continued my intensive job search with little progress; the more I looked and applied, the more demoralized I became. Companies didn't consider me for jobs for which I was qualified or sometimes overqualified. I had dedicated my entire life to prioritizing my education and building a successful career, and now at the age of forty-one, I was unable to find a job or even secure an interview. While Alba and Maia were at school and kindergarten, I started studying online to learn new skills. Every night I took digital courses after putting the girls to bed and

## THE FLIGHT HOME

reading them a story. I studied finance, blockchain technology, digital transformation, inclusive leadership, and any topic that could help me become an appealing candidate. Dave often asked me excitedly whether I had any news, and I was disappointed to say, 'No.' Maybe I wasn't good enough, maybe I had made the wrong career choices, or perhaps there was no place in Australia for someone like me, an outsider who didn't know anyone in the country.

'I'm so disappointed I haven't found anything yet. All jobs require experience and a network in Australia, and I have none. I don't know what to do,' I replied.

'You are already doing a lot. You are raising our daughters, doing all the paperwork, and you are trying your best.'

I sighed. My best was not enough.

As July arrived, I had to look in the mirror. I had already been in Australia for six months, and it was time to face the harsh truth. I had made no progress in my search and had failed to find a job. I needed to change my strategy and my approach but more importantly my mindset. Thinking of Alba and Maia, I asked myself, *what's the story I want to tell my daughters when they grow up?*

I wanted them to be proud of their mom. How could I turn things around? What was under my control? While I couldn't convince the recruiters to give me a chance to show them who I was, I had the tools to build my own personal brand and share my experience on digital platforms. I didn't have to rely on others to build my network; I could go out there and build my own. I realized I had everything I needed to make change happen. What was I waiting for?

One morning I called Dave after dropping the girls at school, and as I said, 'Hi,' he sensed the positive energy in my voice.

'You sound happy. Did you hear back from any of the

recruiters?' he asked.

'Better. I found the answer,' I replied, 'It was in front of me all the time; I just had to look in a different direction.' I paused with a smile. 'If the recruiters don't see my value, I will show it to them. If I don't have a network, I won't sit here waiting. I'm going to build my own.'

Dave frowned like he always does when he's confused. I started laughing and told him I had a plan. I could tell he had no clue, but he replied with a nod, 'I'm not sure what you mean, but you always figure things out, and I'm here to support you.'

That's all I needed to hear from my partner in crime; he was on board before even knowing the destination. Dave's support was the fuel I needed to set my plan in motion.

I hung up and started typing on my Mac. I deleted some words, wrote some more, and an hour later, I was ready to publish my first post on LinkedIn. I hesitated before pressing "Post" because I had never disclosed anything personal in public. I had always shown my side of a tough iron woman who doesn't need any help from anyone. But I decided to talk openly about my journey and struggles as someone facing rejection and feeling alone. I had been through a lot in the past twelve months and wanted to tell my story, motivate others and find the strength to create a new path, even though I wasn't sure where it would lead me. I was afraid old colleagues would judge me, friends would criticize me, and strangers would mock me. I still took the shot. *Don't be silly, I told myself; what's the worst that can happen?*

On July 4th, 2022, my first post on LinkedIn went live.

> *SOS: my world turned upside down. In 2022, I had to unexpectedly move countries, from Hong Kong to Australia, without saying goodbye to my friends. I had to close my newly opened business in China. I had to leave my husband*

## THE FLIGHT HOME

*behind until we finalize what's next. I left my home with my 2 daughters and only 1 purple suitcase leaving all my belongings behind. I have sent dozens of job applications and received dozens of nos.*

*Also, in 2022, I've had the most quality time I ever had with my daughters. I have used my free time to take business Chinese classes and study every day. I am apart from my husband, but we feel more connected than ever because we are a team. I have worked on my self-development and have taken over 20 online courses. I have made new friends and reconnected with old ones. I still have my purple suitcase, but it's now filled with beautiful memories and new experiences. I am grateful for life because it's fragile. Sometimes life will shake your world upside down, but how you react to it is totally up to you! So hang on there and find your purple suitcase.*

After publishing it, I shut down my Mac and went for a glass of water. Seconds later, the notifications started to beep on my phone. First, it was a few, then a dozen, and after a few hours, I couldn't keep up with the *likes*. To my astonishment, the response was overwhelming. That post had over 33,000 views, and I received support and encouragement from all over the world. Friends, old colleagues, acquaintances, and strangers jumped in to give me a virtual hand. The comments continued to pile up, and old contacts sent me private messages cheering on me and saying how I had inspired them. That first step was all I needed to climb out of my hole, start connecting, and reignite my passion for writing and expressing myself. I had forgotten I had a voice and a story worth sharing. My life story.

I continued writing, and in a few weeks, I had created over one hundred pieces of content, had over 2,000 followers on

LinkedIn, and had spoken at my first podcast. After pitching to multiple podcast hosts, the show, *5 Minutes for Me*, invited me to talk about a growth mindset and explain how I had applied it in my life and career to overcome challenges. The episode had hundreds of downloads and positive reviews, giving me the confidence to speak in public and reach out to more podcasts.

With the girls at school, I decided to get fit again and meet people through my hobbies, so I joined the Gold Coast Run Club and the local triathlon club. I was doing the things I loved, meeting people virtually and in person, and blooming again. Mom was right; I had everything in me to be successful and create my own path.

I went on to complete over thirty courses online and started publishing articles on leadership, inclusion, and culture. I was genuinely embracing the privilege given to me—having time off after almost twenty years of uninterrupted work since I started my first job in Shanghai nearly two decades earlier. I had the gift of time and focused on enjoying my mommy-and-daughter time and reflected on what I wanted to do next in my career. I woke up at 4:00 a.m., inspired by new ideas of topics to write about, stories from my childhood, and experiences that could motivate others. I began writing to encourage people to embrace their uniqueness and reinvent themselves. I wanted to transmit my message through storytelling to make people relate and help them achieve their dreams.

One Saturday morning in July, I was having coffee with my mother-in-law, Dianne, in a coffee shop at Broadbeach Waters after finishing our usual Saturday Park Run. Dianne had become my Australian mom, the closest person to me, and I saw her as a friend and a confidant. I was sipping my cappuccino when she suggested, 'Vero, I think you should write a book.'

I almost spit my coffee, choking. 'A book?' is all I said,

## THE FLIGHT HOME

perplexed. She might as well have said to became an astronaut, and I would have reacted the same way.

She went on to build the idea that I should write a book about my experiences with different cultures and languages and my story about reinventing myself in Australia. I liked the sound of it, but I hesitated at first, as I never thought my story was that interesting. Mom had always encouraged me to write a book, as she knew I loved writing since I was a little girl. When I was twelve, I wrote a poem in French in Rio that earned me an award at school. Mom had kept it in a notebook like a treasure, and years later, she wrote the poem on the wall in her home in the Tenerife with a thin brush and black ink. It still lives there as a reminder that true passions never die. That sunny afternoon in July, with no job and no income, I started writing the first page of my book, my story, my life.

My plan of writing online and building a network paid off. In August 2022, I signed a contract to work remotely as a freelance consultant for a diversity, equity, and inclusion company. The founders liked my articles on culture and inclusion on LinkedIn and thought I could add value to their organization with my experience in Asia. All I needed was an opportunity to prove myself, and the moment I had it, my weakness became my strength. My story of failure became a story of reinvention and resilience. Being a foreigner in a new country was now my advantage, as I could see things from a different perspective. The continuous rejection from the corporate world had now opened the door to freedom. I had become a solopreneur on my terms, escaping the corporate ladder. I was writing the book of my past but also the book of my future.

In September, I joined a writers' platform called Medium. My friend Jeff recommended I publish articles there, and I started writing daily. By December 2022, I was no longer the lonely woman without a network. I had built a digital audience of over 5,000 followers, I had spoken at seven podcasts, and I was approached by recruiters and competitors who could now see the value hidden for so long. I was investing in something entirely new for me, my personal brand. I was creating a community around my values and building something bigger than myself. I founded my publication on Medium called *A Smiling World* and invited other writers to join. By sharing my journey and my learnings with others, strangers were coming to me. I discovered I had a voice that could help people, and I didn't want to be quiet anymore, waiting for others to discover it.

It's December 17th, 2022. I nervously walk through Brisbane Airport with Alba in one hand and Maia in the other, with her inseparable toy Pink Bunny. It's been so long since my last international flight. I hope I haven't forgotten anything— passports, check; PCR tests, check; computer and cables, check; activities to keep the girls entertained for seven days in a quarantine hotel ... hmmm ... can't quite check that. That's OK; we will just have to arrive in Hong Kong and figure things out. It will be fine. I check in my purple suitcase, and we head toward the departure hall.

It's been seventeen months since I left my home and life in Hong Kong and started the most random adventure without knowing its final destination. I can't wait to see Dave, Django, and our home, even if it's just for a few weeks. I want to hug my friends, cuddle my stinky puppy, breathe in the humidity in the streets, walk up to the Peak, and fall asleep in our cozy flat while hugging the love of my life.

We still don't have a plan A, and that's OK. We are figuring things out, walking through the maze of life. I finished my book, and I loved writing every single page. It's my story, the story of my nine lives in nine different countries, and the values that

## THE FLIGHT HOME

made me who I am today. It's been a journey of wins, losses, learnings, and everything in between. Now I need to find a publisher, and I don't know where to begin, but that's OK. Like when I did the Ironman, I have to take the first step and show up on race day. So here I am.

I don't know where we will be in six months. Perhaps there will be ten countries; who knows? All I know is that right now, I am in the place I am supposed to be. I always had the pieces of the puzzle in me. I just had to learn to put them in the right place, and now the picture is complete. I looked back, and my dots connected. I found myself and finally closed the loop.

'Attention to all passengers, flight CX150 from Brisbane to Hong Kong is ready to board. Please go immediately to Gate number 8.'

Gate number 8. It must be a lucky sign ...

# Acknowledgments

This book wouldn't have happened without my mother-in-law, Dianne, who convinced me I had a story to tell the world.

A special acknowledgment to my mentor Vicki Bennett who guided me through my memoir with compassion and believed in my potential.

## About The Author

**Veronica Llorca-Smith** is an international public speaker, author and solopreneur. She writes about self-improvement, growth mindset, and cultural inclusion. Her advocacy work for diversity and inclusion earned her the award nomination of Diversity Lead of 2023 by Women In IT Asia. She is a mum of two and a triathlete and currently lives in Hong Kong.

*To leave a review, please scan the QR code or visit the link:*
*https://www.amazon.com/dp/B0CNK1BCVG*

**Previous books:**
The Lemon Tree Mindset
Conquering Your Burnout

www.ingramcontent.com/pod-product-compliance
Lightning Source LLC
LaVergne TN
LVHW041937070526
838199LV00051BA/2828